Foreword

The Sex Offender Register was introduced under the Sex Offenders Act 1997. It requires certain convicted and cautioned offenders to register their new addresses with their local police force within fourteen days of their release from custody or hospital or on moving home.

This PRC report is the first evaluation of police use of the register. It examines issues such as the utility of sex offender registration information, the registration process, force policies and organisational structures, information management and the monitoring of sex offenders. It also provides information on the perceived strengths and weaknesses of the legislation and suggests how it might be improved in the future. This report provides valuable information which should assist the police in protecting the public from sex offenders in the community.

Carole F. Willis
Head of Policing and Reducing Crime Unit
Research Development and Statistics Directorate
Home Office
July 2000

Acknowledgements

Thanks are due to all members of the police service who participated in this study and were so generous with their time and expertise.

Former police officer Elaine Morrison carried out many of the interviews and contributed significantly to the research. Her assistance was invaluable. Thanks are also due to: Ian Clark, Staff Officer to the Chief Constable, Gloucestershire Constabulary; Magnus Gudmunsson and John Fox, HM Inspectorate of Constabulary; Peter Neyroud, West Mercia Constabulary; Norman Trew, Paedophile Intelligence Section, NCIS; Chief Inspector Joe Thompson, Police Information Technology Organisation; Nick Richmond, National Coordinator for Paedophile Intelligence and Robin Fallows, Child Pornography and Obscene Publications, HM Customs and Excise; Stuart Gallimore, National Association for the Development of Work with Sex Offenders (NOTA); Peter Goldblatt and Ricky Taylor, Research Development and Statistics Directorate.

Emma Marshall, Julie Taylor-Browne, Cressida Bridgeman and Ann Deehan of the Policing and Reducing Crime Unit provided helpful advice at all stages of the project.

The authors

Joyce Plotnikoff and Richard Woolfson are independent consultants in management, IT and the law.

PRC would like to thank Bill Hebenton, Lecturer in Criminology at the School of Social Policy, Manchester University, who acted as external assessor for this report.

Executive summary

This is the first study to examine how the police service is implementing the registration provisions of the Sex Offenders Act 1997 which came into force on 1 September 1997. The Act requires sex offenders convicted or cautioned on or after that date, or who were serving custodial or community sentences or were under post-release supervision at that date, to notify the police of their names and addresses and of any subsequent changes. This requirement lasts for periods of time that vary according to the seriousness of the offence but it is a lifetime requirement for anyone imprisoned for 30 months or more. The study was undertaken in three phases between August 1998 and April 1999; all 43 forces in England and Wales participated.

Key findings

The current picture

Most officers felt that, on balance, the Act's contribution to policing justified the effort involved. Benefits included improved quality of information and working relationships with other agencies. Perceived problems included deficiencies in the legislation, inadequate resources for monitoring offenders, fears that resources had been diverted away from other categories of higher risk offender, and the creation of unrealistic expectations on the part of the public and other agencies.

One year after the Act came into force, figures from the Police National Computer (PNC) showed that the national rate of compliance with a requirement to register, which has risen since registration began, was 94.7%. Figures for individual forces ranged between 85.4% and 100%.

Sentences for offenders convicted of failing to comply with registration requirements varied widely, ranging from fines and absolute discharges to periods of custody.

There are no published figures on reconviction rates among offenders with a registration requirement; individual force statistics may underestimate the numbers involved.

Only nine forces (21%) used performance indicators relating to sex offender registration. Potential indicators such as compliance and reconviction rates could be misleading if used in isolation.

Figures on sex offence convictions and cautions are published annually in Criminal Statistics. However, not all of these offences attract a registration requirement and not all offences for which there is a registration requirement come within the definition of a sexual offence in Criminal Statistics. These differences limit the usefulness of the figures in evaluating the impact of sex offender registration. There is no precise estimate for the number of sex offenders in the population who would currently be required to register if the Act had always been in place.

Force policies and organisational structures

Few forces referred to the management of sex offenders in policing plans, crime and disorder audits or crime reduction strategies. This omission was seen as having a significant impact on the status of the work and had consequences for resource allocation.

No single approach to the organisational location of register functions within police forces emerged as clearly preferable. Senior officers saw the key to organisational success as striking a balance between central co-ordination and divisional responsibility. Most forces reckoned that implementation of the Act had resulted in a significant increase in their workload, but only 17 (40%) had provided additional manpower.

Information flow and the registration process

There were significant problems relating to the timeliness and quality of information flow from courts, prisons and hospitals about offenders with a registration requirement.

PNC is the only mechanism for making register information available nationally, but interim arrangements for entering the information onto PNC were widely perceived as problematic. Many forces relied instead on in-force systems. This fragmentation of sources, combined with a lack of systematic quality control on the data held, were significant impediments to the usefulness of the register.

Views differed as to whether registration information relating to offenders living within the area should be notified or accessible to all local officers. Some forces felt that general access was vital to obtain the full intelligence benefit while others controlled access because of the sensitivity of the information. Twelve forces (28%) did not routinely inform divisional officers of the local presence of all sex offenders with a registration requirement.

Monitoring sex offenders

Although the Sex Offenders Act confers no right of entry to the offender's home, almost all offenders co-operated with home visits. Thirty forces (70%) visited all offenders with a requirement to register. A further ten (23%) only visited those assessed as higher risk or who met some other condition. In 31 forces (78% of those conducting visits), frequency depended on the outcome of a risk assessment.

In 25 forces (63%), visits were used to record further details about the offender and his circumstances on a form (usually part of a specially designed risk assessment package) while seven (18%) said it was only to verify the offender's address. Approaches to the conduct of visits could vary at the divisional level within the same force.

Most senior officers viewed the sharing of information with other agencies, particularly the probation service, as beneficial. However, only one force identified itself as having formal links to a community treatment programme for sex offenders.

Almost all forces had a community notification policy but only five had invoked this in respect of a specific sex offender with a registration requirement. Where there was concern about an individual offender, forces were more likely to use general awareness-raising measures within the community, without disclosing individual details.

Training relating to the Act had been provided in 22 forces (51%).

The utility of sex offender registration information

At the time of the study, some forces were doing the minimum compatible with their obligations under the Act, namely maintaining a library of register information, whereas others used registration to develop and act on intelligence packages. However, the level of force activity is likely to have increased since the introduction of the national risk assessment model for sex offenders in April 1999.

Officers attributed much of the failure to make greater use of register intelligence to poor communication within the police service and a lack of accountability for the management of sex offender work in general. Although senior officers in 31 forces (72%) reported receiving feedback from divisions about how register information was used in the prevention or detection of crime, only ten (23%) described the feedback as systematic. Only 13 forces (30%) described instances in which monitoring activity triggered by the register was thought to have contributed to crime prevention and only ten (23%) reported using register intelligence in investigations. Again, the use of register intelligence may have increased since the introduction of the national risk assessment model for sex offenders in April 1999.

Recommendations

On the basis of these key findings, a series of recommendations has been drawn up for consideration by the Home Office, police forces, the Association of Chief Police Officers and the Prison Service:

The Home Office should consider:

- *reviewing the scope of the legislation in light of the concerns raised by the police service;*
- *clarifying the status of sex offender monitoring in relation to other policing priorities;*
- *promoting links between sex offender monitoring by the police and community treatment programmes, along the lines of the Home Office Pathfinder pilot project on sex offender treatment, with a view to lowering the risk and increasing the stability of sex offenders in the community;*
- *convening a working group to revise the notice of registration requirement used by courts and prisons and ensure that the urgency of onward transmission to the police of the completed form is clearly stated. The group should look at the wording of guidance for offenders;*
- *whether guidance is needed to clarify the circumstances in which a sex offender with a registration requirement can be prosecuted more than once for failure to register;*
- *whether guidance is needed for those sentencing offenders for failure to register;*
- *whether failure to register should be an arrestable offence in order to indicate its seriousness and bring it into line with failure to register under the terms of a sex offender order;*
- *reviewing the definition of a 'sexual offence' used in Criminal Statistics to ensure it includes all offences that attract a requirement to register and publishing figures for the number of offenders convicted or cautioned for a registrable offence, the number convicted for failing to register and the sentences they received;*
- *discussing with those responsible for the new magistrates' court (LIBRA) and Crown Court (CREDO) computer systems the ability to flag offences attracting a registration requirement and the production of sex offender register notices for specified offences; and,*
- *liaising with the Department of Health to improve communications between hospitals and the police in respect of offenders with a registration requirement.*

ACPO *should consider:*

- *liaising with the probation service to develop a group of measures which, taken together, would assist in measuring the effectiveness of registration and sex offender monitoring;*
- *assisting forces to develop more systematic training concerning those required to register, sex offenders who are not required to register and other violent and dangerous offenders;*
- *convening a national meeting of officers involved in sex offender monitoring to address issues including risk management strategies, the development of intelligence on sex offenders, the exchange of information about home visit checklists and the contribution of databases to monitoring and crime detection, and the development of relevant training programmes; and*
- *issuing a list, to be updated periodically, of the contact details for the unit responsible for sex offender registration in each force.*

Forces *should consider:*

- *addressing sex offender monitoring in force policing plans and crime prevention strategies; and*
- *conducting a review of key policing issues arising from the implementation of the Sex Offenders Act. The review should address both internal factors and external interfaces with other agencies.*

The Prison Service *should consider:*

- *whether notice to the police of release of offenders with registration requirements should be harmonised with more detailed advance notice requirements to social services about Schedule One offenders (people convicted of an offence under Schedule One of the Children and Young Persons Act 1933).*

Contents

List of tables

List of figures

1. Introduction

Background

The monitoring of sex offenders in the community 'has had a spectacular rise in the market of public concerns and a remarkably quick response in terms of legislation coming on to the statute book' (Soothill and Francis, 1998). The Sex Offenders Act came into operation on 1 September 1997; other related legislative measures include sex offender orders and extended supervision of sex offenders introduced by the Crime and Disorder Act 1998. The Sex Offenders Act requires certain categories of sex offender to notify the police in person or by post of their name and address and any subsequent changes. This contrasts with aliens who must register in person at designated stations where they are interviewed by specialist officers. Sex offenders have a 14 day grace period following conviction and sentence or release from custody before registration applies. Offenders must notify the police of a new address within 14 days following any change, but need not alert the police to forthcoming moves or tell the police if they go abroad.

Registration applies to offenders who are:

- convicted or cautioned of a specified offence as detailed in Schedule 1 of the Act;
- found not guilty by reason of insanity;
- unfit to plead but found to have done the act charged; and
- those sentenced since 1991 who were, on commencement, still in contact with the criminal justice system, whether awaiting sentence, in prison, subject to supervision, serving a community sentence, detained in hospital or subject to guardianship.

Not all sex offenders come within the scope of the Act. If it had always been in force, it is estimated that fewer than half of all men convicted of a sexual offence would be required to register. The need to register is determined by the type of offence, the age of the offender (registration periods for offenders under 18 are half those for adults), the age of the victim and, in the case of an indecent assault on a person over the age of 18, the length of the sentence (adults imprisoned for 30 months or more must register for life). Murder, manslaughter, kidnapping and abduction are, however, excluded even if there was a sexual component to these crimes[1]. At the other end of the spectrum, the offence of indecent exposure does not require registration.

The Home Office White Paper 'Protecting the Public: The Government's Strategy on Crime in England and Wales' described the purpose of registration as ensuring that the information on convicted sex offenders on the Police National Computer (PNC) was fully up to date. This central resource could then help the police both to

[1] *The Home Office points out that these offences do carry the possibility of life imprisonment and as such render these offenders subject to life licence on release.*

prevent crimes and to identify suspects once an offence has been perpetrated, and might also act as a deterrent to re-offending.

The flagging of sex offenders was made possible by the introduction in 1995 of Phoenix, an enhancement of the PNC names application. As an interim measure, a marker placed on Phoenix identifies an offender convicted of a relevant offence as a registered or unregistered sex offender. The Association of Chief Police Officers (ACPO) advised forces to maintain a local database system also (ACPO Crime Committee, 1997). It is therefore misleading to visualise 'the register' as a single, uniform body of information because forces record register information across different databases.

[2] *Home Office Circular 39/1997 is to be superseded by a new circular on disclosure.*

The government expects the assessment of offenders to be undertaken by the police working with other agencies, in order to protect children and vulnerable adults (Home Office Circular 39/1997)[2]. ACPO confirmed that this process should apply to all offenders who pose a risk, whether registered or not, and emphasised that register records should be treated as a 'dynamic mechanism' integrated into risk assessment and risk management systems (ACPO Crime Committee 1997). Even prior to the Act, such collaboration was described as 'extensive and increasing', particularly between the police and probation (HM Inspectorate of Probation 1998).

In the United States, the contribution of registers to investigation and prevention has not been systematically evaluated (Hebenton and Thomas 1997). In this country, registration provisions have been the subject of considerable debate, raising concerns that they have been used to fuel alarmist media stories or conversely, that they create a false sense of security on the part of the public. In 1998, HM Inspectorate of Constabulary sparked controversy by describing the Act as a challenge to proactive policing skills. Because of the large proportion of sex offenders without a registration requirement, Soothill and Francis observed that 'Any assumption that the scheme "captures" the most active sex offenders is untrue. The Act may indeed develop the misleading idea that the greater risks are being identified'. They queried whether the police 'will do the work with vigour or with resistance' (Soothill and Francis 1998).

Aims of the study

The aims of this study were to:

- investigate police perspectives on the effectiveness of the registration provision, both on its own and in conjunction with other intelligence systems, in light of its objective of contributing to the detection, prevention and deterrence of sex offending;

- document policies and practices concerning the processing of registration information nationally and locally, including quality assurance and verification procedures;
- describe the relationship of registration information to other relevant databases;
- examine rates of compliance with the registration requirement and the consequences of non-compliance;
- identify relevant training issues;
- describe arrangements for the disclosure of information held on registers, including multi-agency work; and
- identify good practice, problems and difficulties arising from the interface between the police and other agencies.

Methodology

This study was undertaken between August 1998 and April 1999. The first phase consisted of a national survey in which all 43 forces in England and Wales responded to written questions about the management and use of register information. They also provided copies of force policies and other relevant documentation.

In the second phase, interviews were held in each force with the senior officer responsible for overseeing implementation of the Sex Offenders Act and the officer designated as the point of receipt for registration information (a total of 86 interviews). Most of these were conducted by telephone. The semi-structured interviews for phases one and two were pilot tested during visits to two forces.

The third phase of the study consisted of 50 interviews conducted during visits to six forces. These forces were selected on the basis of their differences in organisational approach. Interviewees included:

- senior officers with responsibility for overseeing implementation of the Sex Offenders Act;
- senior officers responsible for operational policing and crime management;
- personnel with responsibility for the input of sex offender register information onto the Police National Computer (PNC);
- officers with management responsibility for child protection;
- people with day to day responsibility for management of register information; and
- officers who visit offenders with a registration requirement.

During the third phase, records relating to approximately ten offenders with a registration requirement were discussed with relevant personnel in each force. The review of these records was used to investigate concerns raised in phase two about information flow and sex offender management.

The research began soon after an ACPO national survey that collected statistics and assessed the police service experience with the Sex Offenders Act. We therefore attempted to avoid overlap with the questions posed by ACPO. This study was also undertaken in parallel with another Home Office project examining the risk assessment of dangerous and sex offenders. Consequently, this study did not cover risk assessment procedures in any detail.

Structure of the report

The structure of this report is as follows:

- sections 2 and 3 deal with statistics, performance indicators and force policies;
- sections 4 to 6 describe force organisational structures, information flow and information management;
- sections 7 and 8 examine the monitoring of sex offenders and the utility of register information;
- section 9 draws conclusions from the study findings and presents a series of recommendations;
- appendix A lists police responsibilities relating to the registration of sex offenders; and,
- appendix B provides a checklist for reviewing the force response to the Sex Offenders Act.

2. The current picture

Offences resulting in a conviction or caution represent only a small proportion of total sex offending. Registration targets only those offenders who have been convicted or cautioned for a relevant offence and those who were sentenced after 1991. This section focuses on available statistics relating to this group and how these were used to measure performance.

Statistics on the number of offenders with a registration requirement

The PNC provides data on the number of sex offenders with a registration requirement including the number who fail to register. Similar information is available from the databases and manual records of individual forces. Figures from both sources are regularly compiled and compared by ACPO, which reports close agreement between the two (information provided by Chief Constable A. Butler, Gloucestershire Constabulary). An ACPO working group has prepared a User Requirement for changes to Phoenix software (used by forces to enter information onto PNC) that will allow a greater range of statistical reports concerning sex offender registration to be produced, although it is not certain when these changes will be implemented.

The total number of sex offenders with a registration requirement on PNC at 31 August 1998 was 8,608. Of these, 6,262 (73%) had registered; 1,993 (23%) were in custody or were within the 14-day period allowed for registration and 353 (4%) were apparently committing an offence by failing to register. The figure for offenders in custody is an underestimate. Some forces have flagged with a registration requirement the PNC entries of all long-term offenders who were convicted and imprisoned before the implementation of the Sex Offenders Act on 1 September 1997; others have only flagged the entries of those convicted and imprisoned since that date. Therefore, some offenders with a registration requirement who were imprisoned before the Act's implementation and who are still in custody are not included in the total figure.

The police service in general takes the view that a breakdown by force of the number of registered sex offenders in the community should not be published. It stresses the need for careful interpretation of force registration figures because:

- breakdown on a force by force basis of those with a registration provides an incomplete picture of the number of convicted sex offenders living within the community;
- the number of offenders per 1,000 of the population is not constant. The presence of bail hostels accepting sex offenders, treatment programmes and clinics can swell the number of offenders in an area;

- figures are skewed by the fact that many offenders are drawn to the anonymity of densely-populated urban areas;
- PNC data indicates the force creating the original record. As time progresses and sex offenders move, the only way to establish with certainty where a sex offender lives is to read the free text field on PNC; and
- it is argued that publishing registration figures on a force by force basis will encourage media publicity which will have an adverse impact on local law enforcement and the management of sex offenders.

ACPO statistics break down the number of registered sex offenders into three age categories: under 18, between 18 and 21 and over 21. The maximum and minimum proportions in each category in different forces are as follows:

Table 1: Proportion of registered sex offenders by age in different forces		
Age range	Maximun	Minimum
Under 18	25%	0%
Between 18 and 21	13%	0%
Over 21	100%	69%

The figures demonstrate that in all forces the majority of registered offenders are over 21. However, the representation of young offenders among registrants varies between forces. Some report that offenders under 18 account for a quarter of all registrants while others have no registered offenders in this age range.

Although PNC records offenders' ages, it cannot generate a breakdown by age of offenders with a registration requirement. This facility is included in the ACPO User Requirement. It would also be possible to calculate such a breakdown from the figures provided to ACPO by individual forces, but this is not routinely done at present.

Compliance with registration requirements

The data from PNC at 31 August 1998 produced a national rate of registration compliance of 94.7%. Figures from individual forces show compliance rates ranging between 85.4% and 100% on the same date. ACPO points out that compliance rates have risen steadily since registration began, both nationally and in individual forces, although the rate of increase is slowing. However, it could be misleading to use compliance in isolation as an indicator of performance. For instance, if courts or prisons fail to notify the police of those required to register, or if a force is poor at verifying the accuracy of offenders' registration details then the compliance rate could appear to be higher than is actually the case. Such a force could be unaware of offenders with a registration requirement or those who had moved without re-registering and were therefore in breach of the provisions.

Of the 353 offenders identified by ACPO as in breach of the requirement to register, 148 had been unregistered for more than four months. This represented a fall in the number of long-term avoiders compared with the April 1998 figure of 161. The fall may be attributable to increased experience among forces in operating the registration requirements resulting in the use of more effective methods to ensure compliance.

Action taken against those who fail to register

In the first year of the Act, ACPO reported that 67 individuals were cautioned for failing to register or failing to notify change of details. Over 100 people had been prosecuted for registration offences and a further 40 cases were pending. Forces reported a wide diversity of sentences for those convicted of a registration offence. In some areas, offenders had been given custodial sentences ranging from seven days to six months while in others conditional or absolute discharges or fines of between £50 and £200 had been imposed. It was believed that excessively lenient penalties could undermine the extent of registration compliance. Some forces believed that offenders could only be prosecuted once for failure to register. There was confusion about what could be done about offenders who continued to refuse to register following caution or prosecution. However, failure to register under the Act is a continuing offence: once proceedings have been taken, if the offender fails to register, new proceedings can be instituted. One sex offender had been jailed three times for failure to register.

Provisional figures were available from the Home Office Court Proceedings database for the period January to December 1998. They showed that during this period 26 offenders with a registration requirement were cautioned for failing to provide their names to the police and 21 for failing to notify their home address. The results of prosecutions in magistrates' courts are set out in Table 2.

Three offenders were committed for trial to the Crown Court and all three were found guilty. One was given a community penalty, one was fined and one was conditionally discharged.

The figures support the view that courts pass widely differing sentences for registration offences, ranging from an absolute discharge to imprisonment. Light

Table 2: Results of prosecutions in the magistrates' courts for registration offences										
Offence	Proceeded against	Convicted	Committed for sentence	Absolute discharge	Conditional discharge	Fine	Community penalty	Custody	Other
Failure to notify name	95	51	1	3	12	24	0	10	1
Failure to notify address	113	88	2	2	17	51	5	1	2
Notifies false name	2	1	0	0	0	1	0	0	0
Notifies false address	4	3	0	0	0	1	1	1	0
Total	214	143	3	5	29	77	6	12	3

sentences predominate with the vast majority of those convicted being fined or discharged. Only one of the four offenders convicted of giving false details was given a custodial sentence.

Reconviction

Only a small proportion of re-offending by sex offenders with a registration requirement results in prosecution and conviction. Marshall (1994) pointed out that reconviction rates among imprisoned sexual offenders are low compared to rates for other types of offenders. In his cohort study (1997), 10% of offenders were convicted of a further sexual offence and 22% of a sexual or violent offence within five years of their first such conviction. A separate study of offenders against children (Soothill, Francis and Ackerley, 1998) found that over a period of 21 years, 50% were reconvicted of an indictable offence, 20% of an indictable sex offence and 16% of an indictable child sex offence. As Grubin (1998) points out, the period covered by such studies is significant because research evidence suggests that the risk of re-offending by sex offenders diminishes over time more slowly than for other types of offenders. This is clearly important in assessing the risk posed by sex offenders released back into the community.

In response to a request from ACPO, forces identified 56 registered sex offenders who had committed additional sex offences during the first 12 months of the Act's operation. We asked forces what was involved in answering the ACPO enquiry. Twenty-seven (63%) said it had been necessary to check each offender's record individually while 11 (26%) were able to query their database automatically (interviewees in the remaining forces were not sure how the question had been answered). We also asked whether the officer designated for receipt of register information was routinely told about re-offending by those with a registration requirement. Table 3 shows that many were given only partial information and some received none at all.

Table 3: Is your office informed of re-offending by those with a registration requirement?		
	Frequency	Percent
Yes, if new offence is sexual	3	7
Yes, whatever the offence	24	55
No	13	30
Don't know	3	7
Total	43	100

Performance indicators

Only nine forces (21%) reported using performance indicators relating to sex offender registration. The majority of indicators involved counting the number of offenders meeting specified criteria. Examples included all those with a registration requirement, the numbers convicted and cautioned, the number registering within the time allowed, the number in breach of a registration requirement for a specified length of time, the number re-offending and those falling into a particular risk category. Other statistics used as measures of performance were a count of multi-agency risk assessment meetings, notifications received from other agencies and instances of sharing and disclosure of information.

As indicated in Table 3, the availability of data on reconviction rates varied between forces. Even where reconviction rates are known, they need careful interpretation when used as an indicator of performance. For instance, a high reconviction rate might result from a force's superior intelligence gathering mechanisms rather than a poor record of crime prevention. During the study, interviewees acknowledged that the increase in monitoring under the Act might well result in increased identification of offending behaviour. Some offences brought to light as a result of monitoring involved victims who were unlikely to make a complaint. Only one senior officer responsible for implementing the Act identified increased reporting as an objective.

In its 1997 implementation guidelines to forces, ACPO observed that 'The Home Office has not yet notified what data will be required of forces to assess the impact of the Act'. ACPO has proposed 14 statistical questions but responses to ACPO and our own study suggested that forces were not collating all of the information on a systematic basis.

Other sources of statistics

Although other sources of statistics on sex offending exist, the information they provide is limited. The Home Office Court Proceedings database holds some information about sex offenders prosecuted for failure to register. Since January 1998, it has recorded convictions for four new summary offences relating to sex offender registration:

- failure to notify police of name or names;
- failure to notify police of home address;
- notifies police with false information as to name or names; and
- notifies police with false information as to home address.

Criminal Statistics, published annually by the Home Office, gives figures on the number of convictions and cautions for sex offences. However, the number of offenders is not identified and the definition of a sex offence is different from the list of offences that attract a registration requirement.[3] These differences limit the usefulness of the figures in *Criminal Statistics* relating to sexual offences in evaluating the impact of sex offender registration.

Marshall (1997) has estimated the number of known sex offenders based on information about the convictions of 'cohorts' of offenders[4] in samples drawn from the Offenders Index.[5] Marshall produced estimates for numbers of offenders committing a range of sexual offences and also for successively narrower ranges, namely 'sexual offences with a victim', 'serious sexual offences' and 'offences against children'. Using his cohort data, Marshall estimated that 125,000 men in the 1993 population had a conviction that would have required registration had the Act been in force at the time they were convicted. Of course, for many of these offenders the registration period would have expired by 1993. However, for 25,000 registration would have been for life and a further 10,000 had a conviction in the ten years prior to 1993 that would have required registration for up to ten years (although presumably for some of this group also the registration period would have expired by 1993).

Marshall's estimates do not give a precise estimate of the number of sex offenders in the population who would currently be required to register if the Act had always been in place. They do not include female offenders or allow for changes in the population of sex offenders due to death and migration, although he considers that the correction required would be small. More significantly, Marshall is not able to provide an estimate for the number cautioned for a sex offence that would now require registration. He mentions that in 1995 there were 2,200 cautions of males for indictable sex offences but not all such offences carry a registration requirement and some of those cautioned will subsequently be convicted of a registrable sex offence.

[3] For example, Criminal Statistics includes as a sex offence procuring a female for an immoral purpose whereas this offence is only registrable if the female is under 16. Similarly, abduction is a sexual offence in Criminal Statistics but is not registrable. Possessing indecent photographs of children carries a requirement to register but is not a sexual offence as defined in Criminal Statistics.

[4] Marshall drew on cohorts in five selected years from Home Office Statistical Bulletin 14/95, Criminal careers of those born between 1953 and 1973.

[5] The Index is a computerised database of all those convicted since 1953 for offences on the Standard List which includes all sexual offences as defined in Criminal Statistics and all registrable sex offences.

Summary

One year after the Act came into force, the national rate of compliance with a requirement to register was 94.7%. Figures for individual forces ranged between 85.4% and 100%. Compliance rates have risen steadily since registration began, both nationally and in individual forces, although the rate of increase is slowing.

Sentences for offenders convicted of failing to comply with registration requirements have varied widely, ranging from fines and absolute discharges to periods of custody. Forces were concerned that excessively lenient penalties might undermine their efforts to ensure compliance.

There are no published figures on reconviction rates among offenders with a registration requirement. Individual force statistics may underestimate the numbers involved because 44% of officers responsible for registration data are not automatically informed of all re-offending by those with a registration requirement. Only nine forces (21%) reported using performance indicators relating to sex offender registration. Potential indicators such as compliance and reconviction rates could be misleading if used in isolation.

Figures for the number of convictions and cautions for sex offences are published annually in *Criminal Statistics*. However, not all sexual offences in *Criminal Statistics* attract a registration requirement and not all offences for which there is a registration requirement come within the definition of a sexual offence in *Criminal Statistics*. These differences limit the usefulness of these published figures in evaluating the impact of sex offender registration.

There is no precise estimate for the number of sex offenders in the population who would currently be required to register if the Act had always been in place.

3. Force policies and organisational structures

This section examines internal police policies in relation to sex offender registration and looks at the different approaches taken by forces to the management of sex offenders and the organisation of register information.

The police organisational response has been influenced by force size; numbers of eligible offenders; resources; policies concerning devolved responsibility to divisions[6]; existing force procedures for the management of potentially dangerous offenders; and views about whether the Sex Offenders Act related principally to child protection concerns.

Policies concerning offenders with a registration requirement

Internal policy documents

All forces had issued internal guidance to officers although the scope and content of such guidance varied widely. In addition to guidance on the Act, instructions reflected the wide range of police responsibilities on which its provisions had an impact. Issues covered included registration of offenders at police stations and by post, inputting and updating of information on PNC and force systems and conducting risk assessments. A fuller list of around 20 such functions can be found at Appendix A.

Policies on inter-agency risk management

Thirty-seven forces (86%)[7] had inter-agency risk management protocols; in most of the remainder, these were under development. Protocols were not restricted to sex offenders with a registration requirement. Six protocols had been agreed between police and probation only, but most also covered social services, education, health, housing, community services and, in some instances, prisons, courts, the Crown Prosecution Service and voluntary agencies. The title generally described the subject matter as 'risk assessment', 'risk management', 'public protection strategy' or as relating to 'potentially dangerous offenders'. Only two protocols specifically mentioned the Sex Offenders Act.

Protocols on disclosure

'Disclosure' describes passing information to agencies or individuals other than those with whom there is a protocol in place to govern routine sharing of information. The police may initiate different levels of disclosure, ranging from informing a third party, such as a head teacher or housing manager, to full community disclosure. The responsibility for disclosure rests with the Chief Constable, who makes the decision on a case-by-case basis and may take into account the views of an inter-agency risk assessment panel. ACPO has recommended that forces publish guidelines on

[6] *The major geographical and administrative subdivisions within police forces vary greatly e.g. 'basic command units', 'divisions' and 'areas'. In the interests of consistency, this report refers throughout to divisions.*

[7] *An increase since the ACPO survey in 1997 which identified 23 such inter-agency protocols.*

disclosure, taking account of Home Office Circulars 39/1997 (to be replaced by a new version), 45/1986 and relevant case law. Thirty-eight forces (88%) reported having published such protocols.

Policing plans and crime and disorder audits and strategies

The Police and Magistrates' Courts Act 1994 introduced accountability through the publication of policing plans which tell the public what services and standards they can expect and assist in performance monitoring. The Crime and Disorder Act 1998 requires agencies including the police and local authorities to carry out local audits as a precursor to the development of crime and disorder strategies.

Few forces made reference to sex offending or sex offender management in policy documents issued to the public or produced as part of the partnership with local authorities. Ten (23%) included references in the force policing plan, five (12%) did so in the crime reduction strategy and six (14%) made reference in their crime and disorder audits. Only two forces (5%) made references in all three documents. However, several forces anticipated that sex offender issues would be addressed in future versions of policy documents.

Responsibility for management of registration information

In the majority of forces, registration management was a headquarters function.

Table 4: Departments responsible for managing register information	
Forces in which management of the register was a headquarters function	
Central intelligence bureau	33
Paedophile unit	4
Child protection	2
Vice team	1
PNC bureau	1
Total	**41**
Forces in which management of the register was devolved to divisions	
Area inspectors	1
Local intelligence bureaux	1
Total	**2**

ACPO suggested that a lead officer, preferably at superintendent level, should oversee implementation of the Act. In the national survey, the lead officer was a superintendent or above in only 17 forces. ACPO also recommended that the designated point for receipt of registration information should be in the office responsible for overseeing PNC applications and entering case results onto Phoenix.[8] In practice, the designated officer was not necessarily responsible for Phoenix data entry but needed to work closely with those who performed this function.

Irrespective of where they were placed organisationally, those with day-to-day responsibility for the register often commented that they had no official back-up in the event of their absence.

[8] *Sixteen of the 43 interviewees who acted as the designated person for receipt of registration information were civilian police personnel. However, all such interviewees are included in references to 'designated officers'.*

Sex offender monitoring

Monitoring entailed verifying the information received and assessing the risk represented by sex offenders on an ongoing basis. The introduction of local policing plans, sector policing and partnership with local authorities, had all contributed to the devolving of responsibilities to divisions. Given the move towards 'local ownership' of policing problems, the growth of the register and the need to undertake as much of the work as possible with existing resources, most forces had delegated day-to-day sex offender management to divisions. Many forces reported that their administrative arrangements were under review, with the likelihood of more work being devolved to divisions. Only eight forces (19%) retained responsibility for visits to sex offenders in headquarters units responsible for management of the register. Where divisions were responsible for visits, command teams had considerable autonomy and there was little standardisation of approach within forces.

Senior officers saw the key to success as striking a balance between the central co-ordinating role and divisional responsibility:

'We have the right solution: managing risk in the community needs to be done at the local level provided overview is with the intelligence bureau at headquarters'.

Tensions between the roles of headquarters and divisions included:

- headquarters' inability to task officers on division with follow up;
- inconsistent practice between divisions in relation to visits and risk assessments;
- poor information flow from divisions to headquarters;
- competition for resources between divisions and headquarters;

- divisional officers with responsibility for sex offenders having other demands on their time; and
- headquarters' inability to access divisional databases.

The relationship to child protection

Commentators on the Sex Offenders Act often assume that it is concerned exclusively with child protection, though many with a register requirement have committed offences only against adults. Forces differed as to whether child protection units were involved in monitoring offenders.

In the six fieldwork forces, child protection managers said that although their units were encouraged to be proactive in developing and acting on intelligence, they were not 'mainstream intelligence generators'. The managers generally took the view that their officers were not in a position to take on the monitoring of sex offenders due to other responsibilities, even though child protection experience was thought to be relevant.

Three of the six fieldwork forces had organisational links between child protection and sex offender monitoring. In one, sex offender management was undertaken by a force-wide unit of former child protection officers managed by and co-located with child protection. In the second, the officer responsible for child protection units force-wide was also responsible for implementation of the Act; however, he was not the line manager of the officer tasked with day-to-day receipt of register information nor of the officers on division tasked with visits. In the third, response to the Act differed across the force but two divisions were served by a sex offender assessment unit composed of two former child protection officers and a civilian. This assessment unit, which was co-located with a child protection team, was part-funded by a local partnership initiative.

Resources

The introduction to the Sex Offenders Bill stated that there would be no additional resources provided to meet the cost of its implementation.[9] In forces dealing with fewer sex offenders, the work had been absorbed without much difficulty. However, many forces felt that implementation of the Act had resulted in a significant increase in workload.

Seventeen forces (40%) had provided additional manpower. Some forces emphasised that new positions covered only part of the work involved. For example, a force with approximately 300 registered offenders said: 'We have a detective sergeant, two detective constables and one police constable but only one of these positions is new

[9] *Financial and Public Sector Management Effects of the Bill, Explanatory and Financial Memorandum, Sex Offenders Bill.*

and even that is temporary'. One problem with temporary positions was that they often did not have documented job descriptions.

A force with approximately 260 registered offenders which was bidding for one dedicated headquarters position estimated that the work involved '40% of the sergeant's time, three hours per week for the superintendent, half the time of the civilian clerk and half the time of an intelligence officer on each division'. Another force with approximately 100 registered offenders, whose request for two dedicated positions was still pending, noted that 13 people were involved in this work: one disclosures clerk in the central intelligence bureau; five officers involved in risk assessment; five detective inspectors managing child protection; a detective inspector in the force intelligence bureau with responsibility for sex offenders; and a detective inspector at headquarters responsible for child protection. Other forces said requested new staff would not be provided because the force overall was losing civilian and officer positions.

Forces with no additional resources included one with approximately 80 registered offenders. Another force with a similar number of registered offenders had one full-time officer in the force intelligence bureau. However, it described the work as also having an impact on the senior officer who attended multi-agency risk assessment meetings with the detective inspector from child protection, the detective superintendent and detective inspectors from divisions, who met fortnightly to review all cases. Where sex offender management was assigned to existing specialist units without any additional resources, managers of such units described this as an additional pressure in deciding work priorities.

Perceptions about effective force structures

Senior officers overseeing implementation of the Act and officers designated to receive registration information were asked independently about the effectiveness of their force's structure. In 15 forces (35%) both officers stated that the structure in place worked well, while in 14 (33%) both concluded that the structure was problematic. In the remaining 14 forces (33%), the views of senior and designated officers differed. No single approach to the organisational location of register functions emerged as clearly preferable.

In 15 forces where officers agreed that the structure worked well, benefits included:

- consistency in gathering intelligence;
- consistency of initial risk assessment and development of expertise;
- a central point for liaison with external organisations;

- direct contact with NCIS and Customs and Excise;
- a central point for force advice on media policy and community notification; and
- some degree of co-ordination and oversight of sex offender work on divisions.

In the 14 forces where officers saw their force structure as problematic, the principal difficulties involved failure to rationalise the work involved and the lack of a central co-ordinating point. Fourteen designated officers and four senior officers thought that their force response would be strengthened by centralising responsibility in a special unit. Where functions were delegated to divisions, difficulties arose if the centre failed to retain a co-ordinating role:

> 'It's not good enough, nobody gets to grips with it. There is no co-ordination and no formal policy to work to. Devolved policing creates tensions between the divisions and my role in the intelligence bureau at headquarters'.

Fragmentation was seen as time-consuming and inefficient:

> 'We have several different units getting involved and this can be a problem. It would be better to have one centralised department'.

Co-location of relevant departments, where this existed, was seen as helpful, although it did not eliminate the problems altogether.

Summary

Responsibilities relating to registration cut across a wide range of police functions. All forces had issued internal guidance relating to sex offender registration and management. Most had also established inter-agency protocols on the management of a wider range of potentially dangerous offenders and on disclosure of information. However, only a minority of forces referred to the management of sex offenders in policing plans, crime and disorder audits or crime reduction strategies. This omission was perceived as having a significant impact on the status of the work and had consequences for resource allocation.

No single approach to the organisational location of register functions emerged as clearly preferable. In most forces, the headquarters force intelligence bureau managed the register while the day-to-day management of offenders was delegated to divisions. Only eight forces retained responsibility for visits to sex offenders in a headquarters unit. Senior officers saw the key to organisational success as striking a balance between central co-ordination and divisional responsibility. Most forces reckoned that implementation of the Act had resulted in a significant increase in their workload, but only 17 (40%) had provided additional manpower.

4. Information flow and the registration process

Ensuring the currency of information on PNC and triggering of risk assessment depend on the receipt of timely and accurate information about offenders with a registration requirement. Hebenton and Thomas (1997) emphasised that any blocks to this information flow 'will only damage the integrity of the system'. If the police do not receive notice about registration, monitoring cannot begin. The police must match up notices of a requirement to register issued at conviction, sentence and on release from prison to information from offenders who register.

This section describes the routes by which the police receive register information and the quality of the flow of information from different sources as judged by police officers.

How information reaches the police

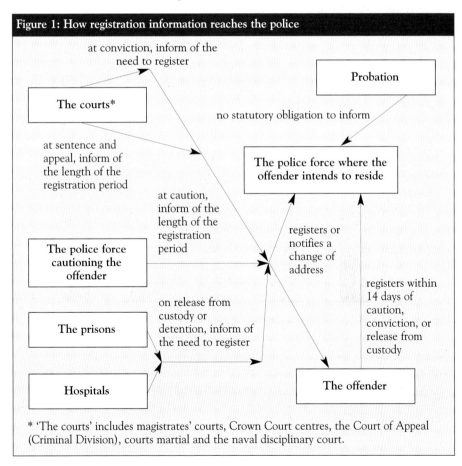

Figure 1: How registration information reaches the police

at conviction, inform of the need to register

The courts*

Probation

at sentence and appeal, inform of the length of the registration period

no statutory obligation to inform

The police force where the offender intends to reside

at caution, inform of the length of the registration period

The police force cautioning the offender

registers or notifies a change of address

The prisons

on release from custody or detention, inform of the need to register

registers within 14 days of caution, conviction, or release from custody

Hospitals

The offender

* 'The courts' includes magistrates' courts, Crown Court centres, the Court of Appeal (Criminal Division), courts martial and the naval disciplinary court.

Figure 1 shows the various routes by which sex offenders need to register comes to the attention of the police.

Reliability

Each force was asked its views about the reliability of courts, prisons, hospitals, other forces and the probation service as sources of information. This covered whether information was sent in all appropriate cases and the accuracy of the information provided. The results are shown in figure 2. It is striking that the probation service, which has no ongoing statutory duty to notify the police about offenders with a registration requirement, was considered the most reliable source.

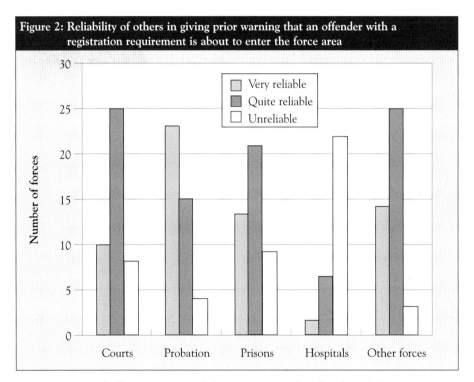

Figure 2: Reliability of others in giving prior warning that an offender with a registration requirement is about to enter the force area

Many designated officers mentioned that sometimes they first heard about a registration requirement from the offender himself.[10] Some indicated that they failed to receive timely notice from official sources in the majority of register cases. Obtaining the necessary information to validate a register entry was time-consuming in the absence of the correct documentation.

[10] *Only a small proportion of sex offenders with a registration requirement are female. For ease of reference, sex offenders are referred to as male in this report.*

Information from the courts

Difficulties experienced by courts in providing convictions to the police were identified by the Home Affairs Select Committee in 1990. Russell (1998) found that no force reported receipt of Crown Court case results within two weeks and some experienced delays of six to 18 months. Thirty-one designated officers (72%) had experienced problems with information flow from courts concerning registration; most had had difficulty with both magistrates' courts and Crown Court centres. A few said they relied on case reports in local newspapers. Problems included:

- courts' failure to serve the notice of requirement to register on offenders who then refused to register;
- serving notice on offenders convicted of offences falling outside the parameters of the Act (in such cases, 19 forces (44%) notified the offender directly that he was not required to register while eight (19%) asked the court to tell the defendant);
- judges who thought they could change the length of the registration period, for example reducing it from ten to five years;
- delays or failure to send certificates of registration to the police following conviction or sentence;[11]
- not faxing certificates to the designated officer;
- certificates not signed by defendants at court;[12]
- poor recording by court staff on the certificate (the lack of full name and date of birth made it difficult to match the certificate with other papers; failure to include the date of conviction and length of sentence made it impossible for the police to calculate the length of the registration period; at sentence, the length of the registration period was sometimes not included); and
- deficiencies in the certificate itself.

The police suggested that the court certificate should include the age of the victim; more details of the offence, as required on the cautioning form;[13] and the defendant's bail status, if sentence is adjourned on conviction.

Some of the problems could be overcome if forthcoming court computer systems highlighted on court lists specified offences for which registration certificates are required.

Information from prisons

Prisons are advised to notify the police of the name, discharge address and date of release of those with a registration requirement when they are 'to be discharged'. This contrasts with advance notice arrangements for the release of Schedule One

[11] *The police and others listed on the form should receive 'immediate service': Lord Chancellor's Department Court Business B3445; B 3464; and B 3490 (1997).*

[12] *Lord Chancellor's Department Court Business B 3464 (1997) Annex D.*

[13] *Appendix B, Home Office Circular 39/1997.*

offenders (people convicted under Schedule One of the Children and Young Persons Act 1933), requiring prisons to give more detailed information to social services departments.[14]

On release, the prison notifies the force where the offender plans to live; if released with no fixed abode (NFA) the prison notifies the force where the prison is located. Prisoners have a financial incentive to claim NFA status, as the discharge grant for an NFA is more than double the sum provided when the address is known.

One in five forces described prisons as unreliable providers of register information. Some prison officers appeared to be unaware of the importance of advance notice of release and prompt dispatch of the registration notice as a 'trigger' to registration and monitoring arrangements. Problems included:

- failure to notify the police about the release of offenders with a registration requirement;
- the lack of a national standard for the timing of the release notice;
- deficiencies in the quality of information supplied, for example the lack of a date of birth, full name or Criminal Records Office (CRO) number;
- lack of information about offenders released NFA;
- sending the notice by mail instead of fax;
- failing to notify the police about periods of temporary release (where these amount to 14 days in a 12 month period, the offender must register);
- prisons' failure to keep the form signed by the inmate advising him of the need to register. Without this, the CPS in some areas has declined to prosecute for failure to register;
- lack of notice about the release of a registered offender convicted of a non-registrable offence;
- failure to identify offenders with a registration requirement because the relevant conviction was not the first index offence;
- lack of information from young offender institutions; and
- the lack of a standard format for the information provided.

Police officers suggested that a standard prison notice should include:

- the offender's full name, aliases and date of birth;
- the date, court, details of conviction and sentence (if a copy of the court notice is not attached), and length of the registration period;
- the estimated date of the prisoner's release, with an update sent if the date changed;

[14] *Prisons must provide details of the release date, reporting instructions and licence conditions: Local Authority Circular LASSL (94)6, 23.9.94.*

- contact details for the offender's probation officer in the community;
- the date when the form was signed;
- contact details for the prison officer completing the notice; and
- advice that the offender's signature did not itself constitute registration.

Forty forces (93%) reported that a police officer was responsible for liaising with prisons. Senior officers wished to see this function used to obtain photographs, estimated release dates and sex offender intelligence such as lists of associates. Intelligence packages developed by forces where liaison officers worked within prisons were considered to be particularly helpful. One force nominated an officer as a link between divisional sex offender officers and prison liaison units, with the aim of tracking sex offenders convicted and imprisoned within the force area and visiting certain offenders prior to their release.

Information from hospitals

Most forces were unsure whether they would be informed about hospital releases because they had not yet been notified of a case. Unlike courts and prisons, hospitals are entitled to exercise discretion in notifying the police about offenders with a registration requirement. Offenders detained in hospital or subject to a guardianship order when the Act came into force were not formally notified of a requirement to register, and hospitals were not expected to notify the police routinely on release. After commencement, hospitals and social services departments were advised to consider notifying the police on release. If the patient withheld consent, hospital managers were to consider whether public interest justified overriding the refusal. Guidance suggested that the need to protect the public meant that the balance would generally come down 'in favour of notification' and recommended that forces establish effective working relationships with hospital managers in order 'to achieve comprehensive notification' (Appendix B, Home Office Circular 39/1997).

Problems included:

- forces not having formal communications with hospitals;
- difficulty in getting health representatives signed up to multi-agency protocols;
- hospitals not providing full identifying information for offenders;
- hospitals bringing cases to police attention but invoking patient confidentiality;
- a doctor who claimed that registration constituted police harassment; and
- private hospitals being unaware of the provisions of the Act.

Examples of improving communications included advance notice of an offender on escorted leave; invitations to officers to attend care planning meetings prior to the release of offenders; and health representatives' attendance at multi-agency meetings on potentially dangerous offenders chaired by the probation service.

Information from the probation service

The probation service has no obligation to notify the police about offenders with a registration requirement,[15] but many forces relied on them as a 'safety net' to notify the police of offenders for whom formal notice should have been received. However, probation officers were less able to flag up cases not under supervision.

Overall, police officers spoke positively of the relationship with probation. Three expressed concerns which included:

- a lack of understanding by some probation officers of the Act's provisions, for example believing that informing the police of the offender's address satisfied the registration requirement;
- some probation officers who did not advise offenders of a registration requirement (although they had no obligation to do so, most probation officers provided this advice and often facilitated the registration process); and
- delays in providing information relating to risk assessment.

Information from the police

Where an offender stays at a temporary address for a period of 14 days, or for two or more periods within any 12 months which, taken together, amount to 14 days, he must notify the police in his home force of that address. When the new address is outside the home force area, the home force should assess the risk posed to determine whether it is appropriate to notify the force concerned of the additional address (ACPO Crime Committee 1997). All but two forces said that they would inform the other force in all cases. Problems identified in relation to information flow between forces included:

- delays in notification of offenders moving into another force area;
- difficulty in obtaining full intelligence such as index files (i.e. the records concerning the conviction) for risk assessment purposes, and printouts from the other force's intelligence system because of data protection concerns;
- inability to identify a central contact point;
- inability to identify who was dealing with an offender on division;
- confusion about force 'ownership' and responsibility for updating PNC records; and
- difficulties in sharing information about good practice.

[15] *The probation service only had a 'one-off' responsibility to notify the police about offenders subject to their supervision on 1 September 1997 when the Sex Offenders Act was implemented.*

Under the Home Office National Standards for Cautioning (1994), before a caution is administered the offender must give informed consent to being cautioned. In cases involving a sexual offence specified under the Act, a person deemed suitable for a caution for such an offence must first be informed of the consequences of accepting a caution. Without this advance warning, the offender cannot give informed consent and the caution is therefore invalid. A form for such cautions was therefore prescribed by statutory instrument, for the purpose of providing evidence in any subsequent prosecution where an offender fails to comply with the notification requirements (Appendices B and D, Home Office Circular 39/1997).

While all six fieldwork forces indicated that officers administering cautions were increasingly aware of the need to use special forms, there continued to be instances of failure to obtain consent relating to registration or to provide the certificate to the designated officer. Some designated officers were unsure about the status of flawed cautions and whether the caution could be re-administered. Some offenders reportedly refused to accept a caution because of the registration requirement.[16]

[16] One force commented that remedial family protection work with parents had been adversely affected.

Sex offender cautions were sometimes processed through police records departments in the normal way without a copy being faxed immediately to the designated officer. Some were only identified when the offender registered, or at the point of PNC entry, weeks after the caution was administered.

It was considered good practice to register the offender immediately after administering the caution. Sometimes this was done in person by the officer on division responsible for sex offenders with a registration requirement.

Information from offenders

Offenders are required to register within 14 days of their conviction, caution or release from custody or hospital, either by visiting or writing to a police station in the force area in which they are living. They must provide their name and address at the time of conviction and any new name or address as well as their date of birth; this information is recorded on a form to be faxed to the designated officer so that the PNC entry can be amended to show the offender has registered. Most forces estimated that three-quarters or more of offenders registered in person at a police station though estimates varied from between 5% and 100%. Problems included:

- gaps in registration information sent by post
- counter personnel in police stations not returning completed registration forms for entry onto PNC; and
- registration of homeless offenders.

There was uncertainty about the appropriate response to offenders with no fixed address who refused to register. Thus an offender who intended to return to work with a fair when his probation supervision ended told the sex offender liaison officer that he did not intend to re-register because he would not be in any location for more than 14 days. The officer was concerned because the offender's previous offending had taken place while in this employment.

Examples of good practice in registering offenders included:

- arranging with the probation service for registration to take place at a probation appointment attended by a police officer or on a joint home visit;
- meeting certain higher risk[17] or high profile offenders on discharge from prison and, by agreement, escorting them to their discharge address where registration took place;
- designated officers attending meetings of counter personnel to discuss procedures;
- asking divisions not to act on forms received at stations until they had been screened centrally, to ensure that offenders had a legitimate need to register;
- sex offender liaison officers based in police stations being called to take such registrations in person; and
- returning registration forms to offenders by recorded delivery or in person as a form of verification.[18]

[17] The terms 'higher', 'medium' and 'lower' risk are used in the ACPO Working Party guidance 'Sex Offenders: A Risk Assessment Mode' (1999).

[18] A copy of the completed form must be given to the offender as an acknowledgement of registration.

Summary

There were problems relating to the timeliness and quality of information flow among courts, prisons and hospitals. The police had not raised such issues on an inter-agency basis. It was striking that the police described the probation service, which has no ongoing statutory duty to notify them about offenders with a registration requirement, as the most reliable source of information. Most forces were unsure about whether they would be informed about hospital releases because they had no formal lines of communication and had not yet been notified of a case. Despite concerns about information flow, examples of good practice in liaising with other agencies were found.

5. Information management

There was no single strategy for the recording and sharing of information concerning sex offenders. Register information was often grafted onto existing police information systems that were only in the early stages of being integrated. Some forces had created a new database to hold sex offender information but this increased the fragmentation of information systems. Forces also differed as to whether register information on local systems was readily accessible to all officers.

Interim arrangements on the Police National Computer

The Act did not prescribe the form in which register information should be held. Guidance from the Home Office and ACPO anticipated that it would be entered on PNC and available to police forces across the country. An interim arrangement enabled an information marker about offenders with a registration requirement to be placed on the PNC Phoenix database. ACPO acknowledged that this interim arrangement was not ideal and that 'some element of local record keeping' would be required (ACPO Crime Committee 1997).

Most forces experienced difficulties with the interim arrangements. The Sex Offenders Act does not give the police powers of arrest for non-compliance. It was therefore problematic that the sex offender register 'marker' appeared in the PNC 'wanted - missing' category, something which officers recognise as indicating the need to arrest the subject. PNC instructions required the marker to be qualified with the words 'arrest only if section 25 PACE applies'.[19] If the offender failed to register after the 14-day grace period, the entry was amended to 'locate - trace'. The section 25 qualifier was often misunderstood by patrol officers and sometimes even by staff in the control room who checked PNC entries on behalf of operational officers; feedback suggested that some offenders had been arrested inappropriately. One force had therefore instructed PNC operators to enter 'Do not arrest' instead of the section 25 qualifier.

Another problem related to the ownership of the offender's PNC entry by the force creating it and the difficulty for other forces that wanted to update the offender's address. The problem centred on the entry of the offender's address on the key 'wanted - missing' page. This page, the most likely to be read by operators, could only be amended by the force that created it. If the offender moved to a new force area, the entry had to be deleted by the 'owner' force and a new entry with the new address created by the force to which the offender had moved. This created a time gap in the record and introduced the opportunity for mistakes to be made in re-entering data. Several forces said that they therefore preferred not to enter an address on the 'wanted - missing' page. Operators then had to look at the address page, which indicated the force that entered each address. The problem is due to be addressed in forthcoming amendments to the PNC system.

[19] Any offence where service of a summons is not practical and where certain conditions apply; for example, where the offender's name and address are not known or are believed to be false, or arrest is appropriate to protect a child or other vulnerable person. Once the condition is satisfied, there is a power of arrest.

The timeliness of data entry onto PNC

Effective register management relies on 'rapid' updating of PNC (Home Office Circular 39/1997). Forces reported that register information was entered onto PNC, on average, within two days of receipt but could take up to 11 days.[20]

[20] All but six forces said they prioritised entry of register information.

In practice, register information was often received at the PNC desk before the underpinning court results and sometimes even before the relevant arrest report. The report carries a CRO number without which a PNC record cannot be created. Data from the Police Information Technology Organisation indicated that forces took an average of 38 days to enter half of their court results onto Phoenix, with four forces taking more than three months to do so. Some fieldwork forces reported that register information would not be entered onto PNC until receipt of the certificate of conviction or sentencing data. This meant that PNC operators and designated officers wanting to input registration information had to chase up the requisite paperwork.

The entry of register information onto PNC was generally confined to one or two people per force or per shift who liaised closely with the designated officer. Where the work was distributed among PNC staff, individual operators had difficulty resolving questions about the length of registration periods.

Force databases

Two forces relied on a manual paper-based system to record registration information. The other 41 used a computer database. Twenty-seven (66% of the 41) used the force's intelligence system (a network available throughout the force area) while 14 (34%) used a stand-alone system. Some forces using the force intelligence computer were considering the development of a separate stand-alone system as register numbers grew. Even forces using stand-alone systems were likely to hold some register information on the force intelligence system or on other force-wide systems such as command and control. It was not possible within the scope of this study to map all the systems within each force where information on sex offenders was stored.

Forces using a database entered register information, on average, within two days of receipt. The longest reported period for data entry was five days.

In 37 forces (86%), databases held not only administrative information but also intelligence on offenders with a registration requirement. In 24 forces (56%), information about offenders with a registration requirement was held on databases containing information on other offenders. Several forces had conducted a special exercise to identify the records on a wide range of convicted and suspected sex offenders, not only those with a registration requirement.

Stand-alone systems

Some of the 14 force stand-alone systems had been developed following visits to other forces and there was a desire for a more systematic way to share expertise in this area. The records of nine stand-alone systems were restricted to offenders with a registration requirement; five held records on a wider range of potentially dangerous and other sex offenders.

Reasons for developing a separate database included concerns about breaches of confidentiality; deficiencies in the force-wide intelligence system (for example, not being able to scan in photographs or to search on the modus operandi of offenders); and the speed with which a specialist database could be developed compared with the lengthy process of seeking minor modifications to a force-wide system.

In several fieldwork forces, divisional officers nominated to manage sex offender information also kept records about visits and risk assessment on a stand-alone computer; access to such information was restricted.

Quality assurance

Data integrity concerns arose because register information was held on more than one system. Russell (1998) found that the majority of forces made no check on the accuracy of PNC Phoenix input and very few forces had procedures for its validation; quality assurance procedures were described as 'few and far between'.

Checks were made in 39 forces (91%) to ensure that information held by the force and PNC was accurate and consistent but only 34 (79%) provided details of the frequency of such checks. Data integrity was reviewed periodically in 21 forces (49%), ranging from once every few weeks to annually. One force had a continuous rolling programme of checks. Thirteen forces indicated that PNC and database records were compared only at entry of register information or if records were updated.

Fourteen forces (33%) acknowledged that record checks had revealed clerical and other errors, some of which went beyond inconsistencies between databases. Problems included registration expiry dates being calculated from sentence instead of conviction; incorrect length of registration for juveniles; unregistered offenders being shown as at liberty when in custody and vice versa; addresses updated on the force system but not on PNC; and offenders registered on division for whom paperwork had not been received by the designated officer. The conduct of a systematic audit was made more difficult by the fact that PNC lists in identification number rather than alphabetical order.

Access to information

Access to register information is important in providing an intelligence return on the investment made by forces in compiling and maintaining the register. In 22 forces (51%), PNC was the first port of call for operational or other officers seeking information about an offender believed to have a registration requirement. This needs to be seen in the context of concerns about PNC access documented by Russell (1998): it was not a high priority for national or local training; it formed no part of detective training or formal induction for constables; tutor constables and supervising officers had little or no PNC training; and operational officers lacked understanding of its functions.

For 14 forces (33%), the primary source of registration information was the force's intelligence system. This was available on a 24-hour basis but, as described below, not all officers had access to it. Six forces (14%) said that registration information would be sought from the unit managing the register.

Some forces placed a 'sex offender register' marker on the address of such offenders in command and control systems and on names in intelligence systems; others decided against this because of confidentiality concerns. As numbers on the register increased, the burden of monitoring and weeding off such markers would also increase and their impact might decline. This was a particular concern in those forces also using markers for potentially dangerous offenders.

Some systems automatically notified a nominated officer when a record was updated; others, less satisfactorily, only requested the officer updating the record to inform a nominated officer. The nominated officer identified by the system was often on division but some designated officers with central responsibility also wished to be updated. Where such designated officers did not receive print-outs automatically, they complained that they were not routinely told about contacts with or re-arrests of offenders or about failure to comply with registration requirements.

Senior officers differed in their views about what information should be generally accessible. Some wanted intelligence on sex offenders to form part of the mainstream intelligence system, thus helping divisions to take ownership. Others felt open access would not be of benefit as their force intelligence system contained little information other than the fact that the offender was registered.

Disseminating information

Divisional officers in 31 forces (72%) were told about the local presence of all sex offenders with a registration requirement; in five forces (12%) they were told about selected offenders only; and two forces provided information only in response to enquiries from officers (five designated officers were unable to answer this question).

The 41 forces with a headquarters responsibility for register information were asked what information they passed to divisions. In 22 forces (51%), this consisted of an intelligence package on the offender; nine (21%) provided basic details about the offender plus the assessed level of risk; and a further ten (23%) said they provided basic details only.

Dissemination was controlled by directing information in the first instance to members of command teams, crime managers, local intelligence officers or other nominated officers on division or to specialist units. It was not possible to identify to what extent front-line officers were routinely notified about local sex offenders with a registration requirement because local practice varied even among divisions in the same force, and designated officers often had little feedback about how this was handled. Factors affecting practice on divisions included views about the confidentiality of the information, concerns about disclosure and whether monitoring was seen as a collective responsibility of divisions or that of nominated officers only. In one force, officers were only made aware of sex offenders if they queried the force intelligence system, which provided basic details only. Risk assessment status was available only through the designated officer. In a second force, officers were only told of an offender's presence if he was assessed as higher risk. In a third force, one division said 'we don't advertise the presence of a registered sex offender unless we have specific concerns and then we put it on the criminal intelligence system'; however, another division routinely briefed officers about all such offenders. In a fourth force where a high profile offender with a registration requirement was monitored through an inter-agency risk management plan, information about him was restricted to senior officers and was not entered on force systems or made known to the nominated officer with local responsibility.

Briefings typically consisted of the offender's personal details, photograph, index offence and assessed level of risk. Instructions were sometimes included, for instance 'do not approach but pass information on sightings to X' or asking officers attending the address for any reason to complete an intelligence report. Paper notices sometimes had a cover sheet indicating the confidentiality of the information but there remained the possibility of access by unauthorised personnel to offenders' addresses. One force piloted an intranet briefing system to pass onto the community policing team information received from headquarters. Dissemination over the intranet ensured that cascading of information was handled consistently and enabled managers to review how often information was accessed.

Summary

PNC is the only mechanism for making register information available nationally, but interim arrangements for entering the information onto PNC were widely perceived as problematic. PNC was the first port of call for officers seeking registration information in around half of all forces; many relied instead on in-force systems. These differed in the extent to which they held intelligence and covered other categories of offender. This fragmentation of sources, combined with a lack of systematic quality control on the data held, were significant impediments to the usefulness of the register.

Views differed as to whether registration information should be accessible to all officers. Some forces felt that general access was vital to obtain the full intelligence benefit while others said that access had to be controlled because of the sensitivity of the information. Twelve forces (28%) did not routinely inform divisional officers of the local presence of all sex offenders with a registration requirement.

6. Monitoring sex offenders

To be effective, registration must be part of a dynamic process in which sex offenders are monitored in the community according to their level of assessed risk. This section examines the ways in which forces have approached monitoring.

Visits

Thirty forces (70%) visited all offenders with a registration requirement, ten (23%) visited selected offenders and three forces (7%) did not visit offenders. Although the Sex Offenders Act conferred no right of entry to the offender's home, forces commented that almost all offenders co-operated with home visits.

In 31 (78%) of the 40 forces that conducted visits, the frequency of visits depended on the outcome of a risk assessment. Offenders assessed as higher risk were generally visited at least monthly (more frequently if their situation was considered unstable) and discussed at inter-agency risk management meetings, so that the burden of monitoring did not fall exclusively on the police. There was heavy reliance, for example, on hostel staff and probation officers. Offenders initially assessed as low or medium risk were not always visited as frequently as specified in force policy due to pressures of other work. Some registered offenders had yet to be visited for the first time. Of the other forces, five (13%) visited at regular intervals of between one and six months, three (8%) left the decision on frequency to divisions and one (3%) visited offenders only once.

Table 5 shows that most forces used a form to structure the collection of information during visits. In addition to routine data, such as a description of the offender's current appearance and details about members of the household, employment and leisure activities, some forms also prompted questions about the interviewee's offending behaviour and knowledge of other offenders. Table 6 shows that it was usually left to divisions to decide who should carry out visits. Percentages are of the 40 forces that carried out visits.

Table 5: Purpose of home visits	
Purpose	**Number of forces (%)**
To obtain information and record the details on a form	25 (63%)
To obtain information but details not recorded on a form	8 (20%)
To verify address only	7 (18%)

Table 6: Responsibility for carrying out home visits	
Unit	Number of forces (%)
Left to divisional discretion	24 (60%)
Force Intelligence Bureau	8 (20%)
Sex Ooffender and Paedophile Unit	4 (10%)
Vice Unit	2 (5%)
Child Protection Unit	2 (5%)

In eight forces, the unit managing the register also conducted visits. If numbers of offenders were small, a local intelligence officer might conduct all visits; as numbers grew, beat officers were increasingly likely to be asked to visit medium or lower risk offenders. Within the same force, approaches varied. Offenders in one division could be visited by specialist plain-clothes officers with a view to completing detailed questionnaires, take a Polaroid photograph, a DNA swab or arrange finger-printing, and in another division by officers in uniform, tasked on a one-off basis and without any specific protocol to follow. Such officers complained that they were not always given enough information beforehand about the offender.

Twenty-five forces (63% of those that carried out visits) indicated that the same officer would visit the same group of offenders on more than one occasion. Officers conducting visits often cultivated rapport with offenders, assured them that their safety and security were important and encouraged offenders to contact them at any time. This approach was thought to result in offenders being more forthcoming when asked about family history, sexuality and offending behaviour. Visits could bring to light changes in the offender's circumstances which might increase the likelihood of re-offending. Some officers referred the offender to appropriate resources in the community. While this did not look like traditional police work, a sex offender liaison officer commented that such action was in police interests as it helped to keep the offender stable.

Several interviewees highlighted the need to ensure that visits were productive intelligence gathering exercises. However, only 11 forces in the national survey (26%) said that officers with responsibility for visits received any training for the task.

Thirty forces (70%) described measures other than visits that were used to verify information provided by the offender when registering (one force stated that verification visits were 'in addition' to regular visits). 'Verification' was interpreted broadly, embracing risk assessment as well as the gathering of intelligence information. Two forces sent letters to offenders and one did this by recorded delivery at six monthly intervals.

Offenders who failed to register

When offenders failed to register within 14 days, PNC needed to be updated to record that the offender's status was 'unregistered - at liberty'. Responsibility varied within forces for flagging up offenders who failed to register. Designated officers in at least 22 forces reported using a manual or computer-based system to identify such offenders: in other forces, it was left to divisions to monitor whether or not they registered.

In most forces, the tracing of offenders who failed to register was undertaken by divisional officers with day-to-day responsibility for offenders. The more proactive visited last known addresses and checked with relatives, probation, social services, housing and the council tax office. One force tasked an officer at headquarters to follow up the small number of unregistered offenders at liberty. He found that some routine checks by divisional officers had not been carried out. A few forces were not enthusiastic about tracking down all offenders who failed to register: one commented that follow-up was 'a waste of time' for offenders perceived to be low risk.

Sixteen forces (37%) had no experience as yet of offenders who had avoided registration for four months or more ('long-term avoiders'). Responsibility for follow-up varied according to the force and the division, and could involve beat officers, crime managers, intelligence officers or those whose sole responsibility was sex offender monitoring. Nine forces (21%) that did not routinely put a marker on PNC for offenders who failed to register said they would do so in the case of long-term avoiders.

Inter-agency work

This study was conducted at the same time as another Home Office research project into risk assessment of dangerous and sex offenders and in parallel with the development of a risk assessment model by an ACPO Working Party. We therefore did not deal in depth with these issues. However, senior officers were asked about the beneficial and problematic aspects of sharing information with other agencies. Their responses, which were generally positive, are illustrated in figure for each of the main agencies.

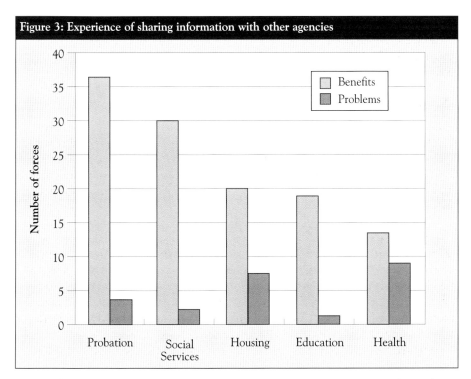

Figure 3: Experience of sharing information with other agencies

The quality of the interchange was highest with the probation service and social services departments. Problems were most likely to be encountered in the exchanges with health professionals.

Home Office guidance observed that Area Child Protection Committees (ACPCs), an inter-agency forum for developing, monitoring and reviewing child protection policies, were 'already expected to include work with abusers in their local procedures, which will in future need to take account of information received [as a result of registration]' (Home Office Circular 39/1997). Fieldwork forces indicated, however, that the ACPCs' relationship to other inter-agency groupings in the post-Sex Offenders Act environment was unclear.

More than half the sex offenders supervised by the probation service and two-thirds of those discharged from prison have not participated in a treatment programme (Cavadino 1998). Forces identified a gap in provision of sex offender treatment programmes, in particular for adolescents, reflecting a concern of HM Inspectorate of Probation (1998) that there was no coherent national strategic approach for dealing with this group of offenders. Only one force identified itself as having formal links to a community treatment programme. When registering with this force, offenders were sent information about risk assessment advising that their level of risk could be reduced by successful completion of a recognised treatment programme, having a good relapse prevention plan and attendance at a maintenance group. The force co-funded a project with Home Office probation 'Pathfinder' status (selected pilot projects designed to examine good practice) to which offenders were referred. In an 18 month period 50 offenders with a registration requirement, including two who had been cautioned, attended the project's two-week core treatment group; advice was also offered to offenders' partners. A senior police officer was a member of the management board. He and agency personnel agreed that the project was a logical extension of collaboration on risk management and made a significant contribution to community safety.

Customs and Excise and NCIS

Thirty-three forces (77%) were in contact with the Customs and Excise paedophile officer covering the force area, primarily through the force intelligence bureau. Thirteen forces (30%) informed the NCIS paedophile section of offenders with a registration requirement. The functions of this section were under review at the time of this study. Responsibility for NCIS contact lay with the unit responsible for managing the register. The register marker on PNC did not distinguish between sex offenders who targeted children. This made it difficult for NCIS to identify the sub-group of offenders against children who had failed to register.

Community notification

In 1998, the Association of Chief Officers of Probation (ACOP) expressed concern about breakdowns in public order and the increased risk of re-offending by sex offenders as a consequence of an unmanaged process where details about individuals had been leaked (ACOP press release 24 April 1998). At least 10% of probation hostels had apparently refused to accept 'paedophiles' for fear of vigilante attacks (Daily Telegraph 29 April 1998). In response to these problems, the Home Office convened a national multi-agency group to assess plans for the release of high profile sex offenders and 'review the arrangements being made for their post-release supervision and media handling' (The Guardian 6 May 1998).

All but one force had a community notification policy for managing the disclosure of information about offenders to agencies and individuals outside those with whom information sharing arrangements are in place (Home Office Circular 39/1997). Seventeen forces (40%) had experience of its use; five had used it only in relation to sex offenders with a registration requirement and 12 had disclosed information on others as well.

General awareness-raising measures triggered by concern about an individual offender in the locality included liaison with community youth groups, St John's Ambulance and schools. In one case, a public meeting was held at which a chief inspector, beat officer, probation officer and sex offender liaison officer provided general information but did not discuss individual offenders.

Organisations to which disclosure had been made included leisure centres, schools and local papers. In these cases, the question of disclosure was notified to the offender in advance, as required by national policy.

Summary

Although the Sex Offenders Act conferred no right of entry to the offender's home, almost all offenders co-operated with home visits. Thirty forces (70%) visited all offenders with a requirement to register. A further ten (23%) only visited those assessed as higher risk or who met some other condition. In 31 forces (78% of those conducting visits), frequency depended on the outcome of a risk assessment. In most forces, home visits were carried out on division. Twenty-five forces (63%) said the purpose of visits was to record further details about the offender and his circumstances on a form (usually part of a specially designed risk assessment package) while seven (18%) said it was only to verify the offender's address.

Approaches to the conduct of visits could vary at the divisional level within the same force. At one extreme, offenders could be visited by officers in uniform, tasked on a one-off basis and without any written protocol to follow. At the other, visits were conducted by officers in casual clothes who cultivated rapport with offenders with a view to completing detailed questionnaires.

Responsibility varied within forces for flagging up offenders who failed to register. Designated officers in at least 22 forces (51%) reported using a manual or computer-based system to identify such offenders: in other forces, it was left to divisions to monitor whether or not they registered.

Responsibility for tracing offenders who failed to register and obtaining their registration generally lay with the officers who managed the register on a day-to-day basis.

Most senior officers viewed the sharing of information with other agencies, particularly the probation service, as beneficial. However, only one force identified itself as having formal links to a community treatment programme for sex offenders.

Thirteen forces (30%) informed the NCIS paedophile section of offenders with a registration requirement. The registration requirement marker on PNC did not distinguish between sex offenders who targeted children, in whom NCIS had an interest, and those who offended against adults.

Almost all forces had a community notification policy but only five had invoked this in respect of a specific sex offender with a registration requirement. Where there was concern about an individual offender, forces were more likely to use general awareness-raising measures within the community, without disclosing individual details.

7. The utility of sex offender registration information

Police forces' responses to the Act differed. Following the first year of experience with registration, forces generally wished to become more proactive, but often felt constrained by lack of resources.

Building intelligence files

For an increasing number of forces, notice of the registration requirement triggered the compilation of an intelligence file either by the designated officer, specialist team or nominated officer on division. Reports were obtained from the home force and others, building a picture of not just the index offence but the offender's complete criminal history.[21] This was often supplemented with information from officers involved in previous investigations, prisons,[22] probation, social services, housing, the Benefits Agency, the utility and phone companies, and multi-agency risk management meetings.

Over time, crime files were archived and eventually destroyed. Some forces asked that sex offender files be exempt from the usual destruction schedules; in order to start the risk assessment process as quickly and systematically as possible, they began collating intelligence information at the point of conviction, even if the defendant was in custody and facing a custodial sentence. Where appropriate, this information could be used to press for the offender's involvement in a treatment programme.

A few forces sought intelligence information from offenders themselves; one invited them to complete a questionnaire at registration which was fed into the risk assessment process. Officers observed that sex offenders were less likely to have information about other offenders than, for example, burglars and their 'fences' because of the covert nature of their crimes. Nevertheless, one officer responsible for visits said 'I always ask if they have information that can help the police. There's a potential to protect with every offender'.

The use of register information in preventing and investigating crime

Forces were asked for examples of how register information was used in the prevention and investigation of crime. Several forces commented that they did not use the information in this way, and some thought that its use was confined to risk assessment. Thirteen forces gave instances in which monitoring activity triggered by the register was thought to have contributed to crime prevention. For example:

- offenders living in conditions where it was thought likely that they would re-offend, for example, in close proximity to children;

[21] *One officer responsible for building a stand-alone intelligence system on sex offenders described only 25% of information held by his force across its various sources as 'easily retrievable'.*

[22] *Prisons could be asked about the offender's visitors, correspondents and associates in prison, involvement in any treatment programme, sources of money and for an up-to-date photograph.*

- intervention with offenders whose activities mirrored their previous modus operandi;
- a situation during surveillance on a higher risk offender in which he approached a young female and the police intervened; and
- a major crime unit taking on a case which would not otherwise have come to light.

Examples of prosecutions arising out of register intelligence included cases involving paedophile networks and Internet offences. In other cases, register intelligence led to cautions or the police working closely with probation to obtain the recall of offenders to prison when licence conditions were breached.

Ten forces (23%) in the national survey had used register intelligence in investigations, although they did not specify whether this had resulted in detections. Six of these forces used a stand-alone database of which four held information on sex offenders other than those with a registration requirement. Investigating officers or force intelligence officers checked reports from crime management and command and control systems and compared modus operandi and descriptive details with information held in respect of sex offenders.

Senior officers were asked whether they received feedback about how register information was used in the prevention or detection of crime: 31 (72%) said they did but only ten (23%) described the feedback as systematic, for example by copies or automatic e-mails of intelligence reports, periodic meetings with crime managers and multi-agency meetings.

Barriers to greater use of register information as a source of intelligence

Awareness of the resource

Her Majesty's Inspector of Constabulary (1997) warned that those who lead locally on proactive policing, intelligence and information sharing may take the view that they have little contribution to make in relation to Sex Offenders Act work. Fieldwork forces pointed to a lack of awareness within the police service about sex offender work, its potential for the development of intelligence and the value of information held. It was not well integrated into the intelligence network or given sufficient priority by those in operational command. Officers responsible for monitoring sex offenders and developing intelligence spoke of the need to 'promote' and 'market' what they provided and to educate officers about the value of the resource. Some forces were still in the early stages of conducting briefings for senior officers about the potential benefits of sex offender management.

Competing priorities

The extent to which intelligence packages generated as a result of registration were used for detecting or preventing crime depended on force policing priorities. Surveillance of sex offenders often involved collaboration between a nominated officer with responsibility for sex offenders, local intelligence officers and beat officers. There was also increasing 'social surveillance' through other agencies.

Even within forces actively generating intelligence packages, there was a concern that the momentum declined or disappeared when police action was dependent on the commitment of further resources. Concerns focused on the inability of the officer developing the intelligence to ensure it would be acted on, and the difficulty in competing for resources with burglary or drugs offences.

PNC Phoenix and the QUEST search facility

Information that can be held on PNC Phoenix includes details of the offender's appearance, accent, associates, vehicles, modus operandi and age of the victim. In some forces, such information was entered onto Phoenix at the point of arrest but was not updated subsequently, limiting the system's use as an intelligence database. The QUEST facility[23] allows keywords describing an offender's modus operandi to be placed on the national database. Twenty-nine forces (67%) said that officers were required to provide information to populate fully all fields on PNC and 27 forces (63%) reported using keywording.

Even where forces had trained QUEST operators on every shift, intelligence officers and investigators often did not know about the QUEST facility, making it unlikely that forces would devote significant resources to keywording. A further disincentive to the use of keywords was the fact that back record conversion onto Phoenix had not included entering the modus operandi. As a result, some forces gave a higher priority to updating local intelligence systems.

Accountability

Forces attributed much of the failure to make greater use of register intelligence to problems of accountability. Their concerns were the lack of use made of sex offender intelligence packages and the lack of accountability for the management of sex offender work in general.

Officers complained about the lack of feedback as to what action, if any, was taken on intelligence packages: 'We send out intelligence and that's the last we hear. We have no clout to say whether the division acts on it or not'. There was a call from

[23] *The QUEST facility (Queries Using Enhanced Search Techniques) is an on-line descriptive search facility for detected offences. The original specification was developed before the registration provisions were introduced. A user requirement has been developed for inclusion on QUEST of a register that will be fully searchable and that will have other practical applications: ACPO Crime Committee, 1997.*

those developing intelligence for greater accountability on the part of those receiving it. It was acknowledged, however, that the police did not generally have procedures to monitor action taken on intelligence packages.

Some officers suggested that the shorter the chain of command and communication between those managing sex offender information and crime managers who direct investigative resources, the more likely that information would be used proactively, for example, where the crime manager was responsible for the sex offender liaison officer and also for decisions to allocate resources for sex offender surveillance. Two fieldwork forces had instituted a system to monitor activity on sex offender intelligence by requesting a written response from divisions to which information was provided.

Fieldwork forces provided examples of how communication and accountability for sex offender work could be improved. In one force, a monthly crime forum was chaired by an Assistant Chief Constable and attended by headquarters crime managers and divisional detective chief inspectors. This forum had already commissioned one review of work arising from the sex offender register and a second, to involve the chief probation officer, was about to begin.

In another force, officers responsible for sex offender management gave a presentation on best practice to ACPO ranks in the presence of divisional management teams, other police departments and external agencies. The questions at this presentation demonstrated the difficulties in quantifying the contribution of sex offender monitoring. The Assistant Chief Constable asked pressing questions about value for money. He emphasised the need to develop data to support cost-benefit analysis.

Some senior officers on division described feeling held to account when they attended inter-agency risk management meetings. However, inter-agency accountability always came second to internal pressures and police performance indicators. As one put it, 'within the force I am only as good as my burglary detection rate'.

Training

Training had been provided by 22 forces (51%). Those trained included intelligence officers, detectives, child protection officers, station desk officers, PNC staff and probationer constables. In 11 forces (26%), training was given to officers who visited offenders and in six forces (14%) to those conducting risk assessments.

Senior officers were asked about training. Three (7%) thought none was necessary. The remainder saw a need for awareness training for the broad range of personnel who encountered aspects of the Act in the course of their work and for probationer constables, and more detailed training for those with specific responsibilities.

There was also potential for inter-agency training provided its content was directed appropriately. The probation service and social services tended to focus respectively on adult and juveniles offenders; training needed to draw on both perspectives and to maintain a primary focus on what was expected of the police. Senior officers hoped that ACPO would provide further guidance on more systematic training across forces in relation to risk assessment.

One force had commissioned an independent assessment of its training which highlighted:

- officers' uncertainties about risk assessment and disclosure;
- the need to focus on practical issues, such as intervention strategies with offenders, rather than on theoretical perspectives;
- the need for supervisors to be trained;
- that few officers understood the implications of the multi-agency approach; and
- the need for a forum to exchange information and obtain peer support.

Perceptions of the Act's effectiveness

Thirty-six senior officers (84%) and 34 designated officers (79%) responsible for implementing the Sex Offenders Act felt that, on balance, its contribution to policing justified the effort involved in its enforcement. The principal benefits cited were increased quality of information and better inter-agency working relationships. Although registration itself was not seen as a significant crime prevention measure, most officers believed that the monitoring associated with registration contributed to crime prevention.

Twenty-nine designated officers (67%) and 31 senior officers (72%) cited problems with the legislation. These included:

- registration being based on the index offence, omitting offences that are not explicitly sexual (such as murder) even though the motivation may be sexual or a sexual assault may have been involved;
- offenders convicted by an overseas court who are not covered on return to the UK;[24]

[24] However, service personnel are subject to registration if convicted overseas at a court martial under a relevant Service Act.

- the omission of offenders who receive a conditional discharge and those convicted of indecent exposure and of indecent assault on an adult if sentenced to less than 30 months imprisonment;
- the length of time allowed to offenders before they are required to register;
- the lack of powers in relation to offenders who travel abroad;
- the fact that offenders are obliged to notify a change of address only after they have moved;
- the lack of a power of arrest for failure to register;
- allowing offenders to register by post;
- allowing offenders with a registration requirement to be released from prison with no fixed abode; and
- the imposition of inadequate penalties for non-registration.

Nineteen designated officers (44%) and 21 senior officers (49%) identified inadequate resources as the principal problem with implementing the Act. They were concerned about the increasing demand on resources as register numbers grew and the knock-on effect on other areas of policing. Competition for resources was made more difficult by a lack of direction about the priority of this work. It was not a Home Office or force key objective or part of the force crime strategy or policing plan. As one senior officer put it: 'How much priority does this actually have? I could live with it as one of the 'top three' objectives but mine are drugs, youth crime and burglary'.

Six designated officers (14%) and four senior officers (9%) felt that the effort involved in implementing the Act was not justified (the remaining interviewees were unsure). Those who felt that the disadvantages outweighed the benefits were concerned about resources being diverted away from higher risk sex offenders who did not have a registration requirement. Some questioned whether the focus on offenders with a registration requirement could be justified if it meant 'robbing Peter to pay Paul'. They feared that sex offenders now received disproportionate attention and were unsure whether the effort expended was justified.

One crime manager observed that:

> 'If we are going to take on sex offender monitoring, we have to have the resources to deal with it. No-one has thought of the full operational implications. You can't gather the information, feed it out and just hope that someone will deal with it. This work calls for specialist officers who can be proactive in support of the districts and conduct their own investigations, because it is hard to devote resources to this in terms of day-to-day policing'.

The converse view was put by a senior officer in another force:

> 'Our Chief Constable will never give sufficient resources to a specialist unit. We emphasise to divisions that they must own the risk of these convicted criminals who will re-offend and that they must target them appropriately. This is not an area of crime that is beyond the division's remit; these are not street-wise offenders'.

All fieldwork forces had experience of lengthy and resource-intensive child protection enquiries into care homes or schools. Officers pointed out that if more systematic attention was paid to the early identification and monitoring of sex offenders, the need for such enquiries could be greatly reduced. One fieldwork force carrying out a historical enquiry jointly with other forces had calculated the costs as £189,000 per force.

Seven senior officers (16%) were concerned that the Act had created unrealistic expectations on the part of the public and other agencies as to the level of control that the police could exert over the movements and activities of sex offenders.

Summary

Forces had responded to their responsibilities under the Act in different ways. Some were doing the minimum compatible with their obligations under the Act, namely maintaining a library of register information. Other forces used registration to develop and act on intelligence packages. There was a general lack of awareness within the police service about sex offender work, its potential for the development of intelligence and the value of information held. Training relating to the Act had been provided in only 22 forces (51%).

Officers attributed much of the failure to make greater use of register intelligence to poor communication and a lack of accountability for the management of sex offender work in general. Although senior officers in 31 forces (72%) reported receiving feedback from divisions about how register information was used in the prevention or detection of crime, only ten (23%) described the feedback as systematic. The intelligence value of registration information on PNC was felt to be constrained by the effectiveness of Phoenix search facilities. Only 13 forces (30%) described instances in which monitoring activity triggered by the register was thought to have contributed to crime prevention and only ten (23%) reported using register intelligence in investigations.

Nevertheless, most officers felt that, on balance, the Act's contribution to policing justified the effort involved in its enforcement. Benefits included improved quality of information and working relationships with other agencies. On the other hand, perceived problems included deficiencies in the legislation, inadequate resources for monitoring offenders, fears that resources had been diverted away from other categories of higher risk offender, and the creation of unrealistic expectations on the part of the public and other agencies.

8. Conclusions and recommendations

Revisiting the Sex Offender Act 1997

Most officers in the study felt that, on balance, the Act's contribution to policing justified the extra work involved. Benefits included improved quality of information and working relationships with other agencies. In addition one year after the Act came into force, figures from the Police National Computer (PNC) showed that the national rate of compliance with a requirement to register, which has risen since registration began, was 94.7%. Figures for individual forces ranged between 85.4% and 100%.[25] The study also revealed widespread police concern about the scope of the Sex Offenders Act, the procedures for registering offenders, the powers available to the police seeking to enforce registration requirements and the penalties available to and imposed by the courts when dealing with failure to register.

Under the Act, the onus lies with the police to carry out checks on offenders with a registration requirement but there is no obligation on the offender to cooperate or even speak to the officer making the enquiry. Non-cooperation has not proved a significant problem to date although there are a small proportion of offenders, including those with an itinerant lifestyle, who have refused to register. Some officers fear that compliance may suffer as word spreads that the Act has few 'teeth'.

There is also a concern that opportunities for intelligence gathering are being missed. Offenders can opt to register by post. Those choosing this method do not have to fill in a form and ACPO has concerns that registration by post makes it impossible for police to verify the registrant's identity. Even where offenders register in person, problems have arisen with the processing of registration forms by enquiry office staff in police stations. ACPO proposals for revising the legislation include imposing on sex offenders registration obligations similar to those that apply to aliens and holders of firearm certificates. These include registration in person at designated stations with trained staff and a requirement to re-register periodically. ACPO acknowledges that these measures have additional resource implications for the police service.

Anticipated growth

The number of sex offenders in the community with a registration requirement, currently around 7,000, is likely to increase for some time to come. As discussed in section 2, there is no precise estimate available for the size to which the register might grow in the future, but a conservative calculation using the figures from Marshall's cohort study suggests that the number of offenders in the community who are required to register could rise to around 25,000, even if there is no increase in conviction rates. Extrapolating from current rates, we might also expect that

[25] *Factors to be borne in mind when interpreting these figures are described in section 2.*

approximately 1,300 of these offenders would be in breach of a registration requirement; however, the number failing to register has actually been falling since the Act came into force and an estimate of 1,000 non-registrants in the future is probably more realistic.

New registrants currently number around 4,000 a year, although names will start to come off the register from March 2000 as registration periods end. In September 2002, the minimum registration period for adults of five years will have elapsed since the Act came into force and the number of names coming off the list each year will increase to about one third of new registrants. This proportion should increase in subsequent years until an approximate 'steady state' is reached in which the annual number of new registrants roughly equals the number whose period of registration comes to an end. However, because a significant number of offenders attract a lifetime registration requirement, it could be many years before a steady state is reached.

The status of sex offender monitoring

Lessons about the operation of registration need to be consolidated quickly in light of the expected increase in the size of the register over the next few years. This study suggests that the police service is unclear about the status of sex offender monitoring in relation to national policing objectives such as reducing burglary. The government and ACPO need to clarify where monitoring sex offenders sits in the list of national priorities.

It is important that risk assessment and monitoring do not focus solely on offenders with a registration requirement but also take account of offenders with no registration requirement who may present greater risks. Some officers expressed concern that disproportionate efforts were being devoted to those with a registration requirement. Databases that cover only those with a registration requirement are less useful for intelligence purposes.

Measures of effectiveness

Forces had no agreed way of quantifying the contribution of sex offender monitoring to improving community safety. In some forces, senior officers had asked for measures to be developed to support cost-benefit analysis ('Best Value'). No single measure of effectiveness emerged from this study as suitable for performance measurement. Rates of registration compliance and reconviction needed careful interpretation.

The development of evaluation measures concerning registration is further complicated by the role of risk management partnerships with other agencies and inter-agency initiatives concerning potentially dangerous offenders who are not required to register. These collaborative areas of work do not easily lend themselves to measurement by conventional key performance indicators.

Training

Training related to the national risk assessment model followed its introduction in April 1999. However, there remains a need for a more systematic approach to training those dealing with registration in the course of their work such as police station counter staff, inspectors who administer cautions, PNC personnel and managers of surveillance units. More specific training was needed for those:

- managing register information;
- visiting sex offenders;
- responsible for child protection investigations;
- with prison liaison responsibility; and
- responsible for developing, evaluating and acting on sex offender intelligence.

In addition to implementing the Sex Offenders Act, many officers were also likely to be dealing with potentially dangerous offenders other than those with a registration requirement.

The need for a holistic approach

Police forces responded to the Act in different ways depending on the extent to which forces saw their responsibilities under the Act as:

- maintaining a library of register information;
- using the register as a prompt to risk assessment;
- developing intelligence on sex offenders; or
- acting on intelligence packages.

Although some forces had begun to review and refine their register and monitoring operations, none were looking at the totality of the response. Many of the problems occurred at the interfaces between the individual components of the response within and outside the force. For example, designated officers often failed to make use of police officers responsible for court liaison or local inter-agency groups for raising problems about unreliable information flow.

Registration and monitoring cut across many functions within the police service. There is a need to bridge the differing perspectives of headquarters and divisions and to put in place appropriate and accountable management structures. The effectiveness of the force approach itself needs to be monitored.

As a first step towards achieving these aims, forces should undertake a review of all aspects of their response to implementing the Sex Offenders Act, including their relationship with other agencies. Detailed topics that such a review might address are listed at Appendix B. At a thematic level, the review should look at the following issues.

Internal

- the strengths and weaknesses of current organisational arrangements;
- whether there is a need for greater specialisation or more devolving of responsibilities;
- the resource implications and where the greatest pressure on resources occurs;
- the range of databases in which sex offender information is recorded, the degree to which this leads to fragmentation of intelligence and the need for quality assurance;
- ways to improve the effectiveness of monitoring, e.g. by the use of a standard form for recording intelligence information on home visits;
- the contribution of sex offender intelligence to crime prevention and detection;
- whether the utility of information is constrained by limitations on data accessibility; and
- how to raise awareness within forces of intelligence information gathered as a result of sex offender monitoring.

External

- problems with sex offender register information flows with other relevant agencies;
- bringing to the courts' attention instances where a register notice has been issued incorrectly;
- the scope for wider use of the prison liaison initiatives;
- points of contact with the National Health Service and hospitals where sex offenders may be detained; and
- the relationship between Area Child Protection Committees (ACPCs) and other inter-agency groups on sex offender risk management, particularly in light of the ACPC's key role in inter-agency training.

Recommendations

The study identified a number of areas where action could facilitate the implementation of the Act and increase its effectiveness.

The Home Office *should consider:*

- *reviewing the scope of the legislation in light of the concerns raised by the police service;*
- *clarifying the status of sex offender monitoring in relation to other policing priorities;*
- *promoting links between sex offender monitoring by the police and community treatment programmes, along the lines of the Home Office Pathfinder pilot project on sex offender treatment, with a view to lowering the risk and increasing the stability of sex offenders in the community;*
- *convening a working group to revise the notice of registration requirement used by courts and prisons and ensure that the urgency of onward transmission to the police of the completed form is clearly stated. The group should look at the wording of guidance for offenders;*
- *whether guidance is needed to clarify the circumstances in which a sex offender with a registration requirement can be prosecuted more than once for failure to register;*
- *whether guidance is needed for those sentencing offenders for failure to register;*
- *whether failure to register should be an arrestable offence in order to indicate its seriousness and bring it into line with failure to register under the terms of a sex offender order;*
- *reviewing the definition of a 'sexual offence' used in Criminal Statistics to ensure it includes all offences that attract a requirement to register and publishing figures for the number of offenders convicted or cautioned for a registrable offence, the number convicted for failing to register and the sentences they received;*
- *discussing with those responsible for the new magistrates' court (LIBRA) and Crown Court (CREDO) computer systems the ability to flag offences attracting a registration requirement and the production of sex offender register notices for specified offences; and*
- *liaising with the Department of Health to improve communications between hospitals and the police in respect of offenders with a registration requirement.*

ACPO *should consider:*

- *liaising with the probation service to develop a group of measures which, taken together, would assist in measuring the effectiveness of registration and sex offender monitoring;*
- *assisting forces to develop more systematic training concerning those required to register, sex offenders who are not required to register and other violent and dangerous offenders;*
- *convening a national meeting of officers involved in sex offender monitoring to address issues including risk management strategies, the development of*

intelligence on sex offenders, the exchange of information about home visit checklists and the contribution of databases to monitoring and crime detection, and the development of relevant training programmes; and

- *issuing a list, to be updated periodically, of the contact details for the unit responsible for sex offender registration in each force.*

Forces *should consider:*

- *addressing sex offender monitoring in force policing plans and crime prevention strategies; and*
- *conducting a review of key policing issues arising from the implementation of the Sex Offenders Act. The review should address both internal factors and external interfaces with other agencies.*

The Prison Service *should consider:*

- *whether notice to the police of release of offenders with registration requirements should be harmonised with more detailed advance notice requirements to social services about Schedule One offenders (people convicted of an offence under Schedule One of the Children and Young Persons Act 1933).*

References

Association of Chief Officers of Probation (1998) *Recent cases of public disorder around sex offenders which have impeded surveillance and supervision.* Association of Chief Officers of Probation.

Association of Chief Police Officers Crime Committee (1997) *Sex Offenders Act 1997 Implementation Guidelines.* Association of Chief Police Officers.

Association of Chief Police Working Party (1999) *Sex Offenders: A Risk Assessment Model.* Association of Chief Police Officers.

Cavadino, P. (29 September 1998) *'Protecting the Public and the sex offender'.* The Times.

Grubin, D. (1998) *Sex Offending Against Children: Understanding the Risk.* Home Office Police Research Series Paper 99.

Hebenton, B. and Thomas, T. (1997) *Keeping Track? Observations on Sex Offender Registers in the U.S.* Home Office Police Research Group Crime Detection and Prevention Series Paper 83.

HM Inspectorate of Probation (1998) *Exercising Constant Vigilance: The Role of the Probation Service in Protecting the Public from Sex Offenders.* Report of a Thematic Inspection. Home Office.

HM Inspectorate of Constabulary (1999) *Child Protection. Thematic Inspection.* Home Office.

Home Affairs Select Committee (1990) *Criminal Records.* Third Report, Session 1989-90.

Home Office (1996) *Protecting the Public: The Government's Strategy on Crime in England and Wales.* White Paper. Home Office.

Home Office (1996) *Sentencing and Supervision of Sex Offenders.* Consultation document. Home Office.

Home Office Circular 39/1997 *Sex Offenders Act 1997.* Home Office.

Lord Chancellor's Department (August, September, October, November 1997; May 1998) *Court Business items on Sex Offenders Act 1997.* Lord Chancellor's Department.

Marshall, P. (1994) *Reconviction of imprisoned sexual offenders.* Home Office Research and Statistics Department Research Bulletin No. 36.

Marshall, P. (1997) *The Prevalence of Convictions for Sexual Offending.* Research Findings No. 55, Home Office Research and Statistics Directorate.

Plotnikoff, J. and Woolfson, R. (1999) *Policing Domestic Violence: Effective Organisational Structures.* Home Office Police Research Series Paper 100.

PMG Ltd. *Criminal Justice Management* (March 1999).

Russell, J. (1998) *Phoenix Data Quality.* Home Office Police Research Group Special Interest Series Paper 11.

Soothill K., Francis B. and Ackerley E. *Paedophilia and Paedophiles* New Law Journal, 12 June 1998.

Soothill K. and Francis B. *Poisoned chalice or just deserts? (The Sex Offenders Act 1997)* Journal of Forensic Psychiatry, Vol 9 No 2 September 1998.

Soothill K. and Walby S. (1991) *Sex Crime In the News.* London: Routledge.

Appendix A: Police responsibilities relating to the registration of sex offenders

- Registration of offenders at police stations and by post
- notice of register information from courts, prisons and probation
- warning offenders about registration prior to caution
- filing original source documents
- inputting and updating of information on PNC, force intelligence systems and separate sex offender databases
- creating and monitoring the use of 'markers' on addresses or names on force command and control or other systems, so that officers are aware of the register requirement when visiting the address or having contact with the offender
- monitoring and following up failure to register
- collating statistics relating to offenders with a registration requirement
- building intelligence files from sources within the police and from external agencies
- conducting and reviewing risk assessments
- attending multi-agency risk management meetings
- responding to requests for information concerning the vetting of employees to work with children
- briefing patrol officers about local sex offenders
- monitoring sex offenders through visits and by other means
- referring sex offenders to community resources
- intervening to reduce the risks posed by sex offenders
- notifying nominated officers about the actions of sex offenders, including re-offending
- assessing when community disclosure may be necessary
- weeding sex offender markers off systems when the registration period expires.

Appendix B: Checklist for reviewing the force response to the Sex Offenders Act

The study indicated that it would be helpful if forces monitored their response to the Sex Offenders Act in totality, that is by looking at all the individual components and the interfaces between them. Many of the problems occur at these interfaces. This checklist suggests topics that might be addressed in such a review.

Policy and practice guidance

- Are internal guidance documents up-to-date?
- Is guidance provided for each aspect of the work of administering the register and managing of sex offenders?
- Does the force have a policy on inter-agency risk management and a protocol on disclosure?
- Is sex offender management referred to policing plans, crime and disorder audits or crime reduction strategy?

Organisational structure

- ACPO recommended that the lead officer on the Act should be at superintendent level. Are there any issues about the level at which lead responsibility has been placed? Does the officer have responsibility for co-ordinating sex offender work across the force? If not the lead officer, does anyone have such responsibility?
- Does the person with administrative responsibility for the register have an accurate job description? Is there back-up for this person? Is this a position suitable for a civilian ?
- Is responsibility for entry onto PNC of register data confined to one or two people who can build up expertise on this issue and liaise closely with the person responsible for the register?
- How many people are involved in building intelligence files on sex offenders? Is there a standard procedure to follow? Is practice reasonably consistent across the force?
- How many people are involved in initial risk assessment of sex offenders? How many are involved in ongoing risk assessment? Does the force follow the ACPO guidance and if not, what procedures are used? Is practice reasonably consistent across the force?
- Is there a central point for liaison with external organisations? Where does this responsibility lie?
- Is there a central point for force advice on media policy and community notification? Where does this responsibility lie?
- Are there regular meetings for those across the force carrying out risk assessment and management of sex offenders, including visits?

APPENDIX B

- What resources are currently involved in all aspects of sex offender work?
- Has the force calculated what resources will be involved in managing offenders with a registration requirement as their number grows?

Information flow

- Examine a sample of register records. Are they date stamped on receipt? Consider:
- the proportion in which the first notice received by the force is from the offender, not from the court or prison;
- whether magistrates' courts/ the Crown Court send all notices at conviction and at sentence;
- whether notices are faxed within 24 hours, as suggested by ACPO guidance;
- whether notices are completed correctly and whether they are signed by the offender;
- whether communication problems have resulted in dependence on information from alternative sources such as court results, and the amount of police time taken up in chasing information that should be provided automatically by the courts;
- whether courts serve the notice to register inappropriately and the nature of the errors;
- what action is taken by the police when such errors are identified and who is responsible for notifying the offender;
- whether problems of information flow or errors in issuing notices been brought to the court's attention and, if so, with what result;
- whether prisons provide advance notice of release for offenders with a registration requirement (e.g. by faxing a notice not yet signed by the offender two weeks before the release date) and if not, how quickly do they notify the police;
- what information is provided by prisons (e.g. CRO and reporting instructions);
- the proportion of offenders with a registration requirement released from prison with no fixed abode;
- the contribution of prison liaison officers to information flow;
- whether notice has been received from a hospital and whether there are formal lines of communication with health representatives (e.g. their attendance at inter-agency risk management meetings and police representation at care planning meetings prior to the release of offenders);
- whether problems relating to information flow with other forces have been identified;
- whether consent is obtained to a registration requirement prior to caution and whether cautions are notified immediately to the designated officer;
- whether forms completed at police stations are sent immediately to the designated officer.

Information management

- Does entry of the sex offender register marker onto PNC have priority over other work? How long does it take, on average? Is entry of register information delayed by waiting for court results or other information?
- Which system is regarded as the primary source of information on offenders with a registration requirement?
- How many force databases hold some aspect of information on offenders with a register requirement (e.g. marker on command and control; intelligence systems; stand-alone systems at headquarters and on divisions; intranet briefing systems)? What purpose does each serve in relation to sex offenders? Who has access to these systems? Is access limited (e.g. by security procedures, insufficient terminals or lack of training) or available less than 24 hours a day?
- What resources are involved in updating systems with information on offenders with a registration requirement?
- Are quality assurance checks made on the data held by the different systems? What is their frequency? What problems, if any, have they revealed?
- If offender records are updated (e.g. with intelligence or information about a stop or arrest), is notification sent to a nominated officer on division and the designated officer responsible for the force register?
- What is the force policy on letting front-line officers know about offenders with a registration requirement and to what extent is this tempered by concerns about inappropriate disclosure? Is dissemination practice consistent across divisions? By whom and to whom is information dissemination? What is disseminated?

The monitoring of sex offenders

- Does the force have a policy that relates the assessed level of risk to the frequency of visits? Which officers conduct visits? Is there continuity (i.e. the same officer visits the offender on different occasions)? Is there a standard format/checklist for seeking and recording information relating to visits? Are offenders advised about community treatment programmes? Are visits used as an opportunity to take photos, DNA samples and fingerprints? Are offenders asked about offending by others? Do officers conducting visits receive training and meet together to pool their experience?
- What other steps are taken to verify registration information supplied by offenders, e.g. letters to offenders?
- Is there a consistent approach to these tasks across the force?

Conclusions and recommendations arising from the review

- Has guidance been disseminated effectively?

- Consider the effectiveness of the organisational structure and where in the force responsibility lies for the various aspects of sex offender work. Can it be rationalised in any way? What is the impact of current resource allocation on the effectiveness of the work carried out?
- How should information flow problems with courts, prisons and hospitals best be addressed?
- Are changes needed to the accessibility of information?
- Which policies need to be updated?
- Have problems identified been fed back into training/ guidance?

Policing and Reducing Crime Unit

Police Research Series papers

114. **Missing Presumed...? The police response to missing persons.** Geoff Newiss. 1999.

115. **Interviewing Child Witnesses under the Memorandum of Good Practice: A research review.** Graham M. Davies and Helen L. Westcott. 1999.

116. **Best Value Policing: Making preparations.** Adrian Leigh, Gary Mundy and Rachel Tuffin. 1999.

117. **The Nature and Extent of Construction Plant Theft.** Alaster Smith and Ruth Walmsley. 1999.

118. **Street Business: The links between sex and drug markets.** Tiggey May, Mark Edmunds and Michael Hough. 1999.

119. **Vehicle Crime Reduction: Turning the corner.** Joanna Sallybanks and Rick Brown. 1999.

120. **The Effective Use of the Media in Serious Crime Investigations.** Andy Feist. 2000.

121. **Policing Diversity: Lessons from Lambeth.** A. Benjamin Spencer and Michael Hough. 2000.

122. **The Effective Detective: Identifying the skills of an effective SIO.** Nicky Smith and Conor Flanagan. 2000.

123. **Policing Anti-Social Behaviour**. Nick Bland and Tim Read. 2000.

124. **Feasibility of an Independent System for Investigating Complaints Against the Police.** KPMG. 2000.

125. **Stopping Traffic: Exploring the extent of, and responses to, trafficking in women for sexual exploitation in the UK.** Liz Kelly and Linda Regan. 2000.

Crime Reduction Research Series papers

1. **Burglary Prevention: Early lessons from the Crime Reduction Programme.** Nick Tilley, Ken Pease, Mike Hough and Rick Brown. 1999.

2. **Neighbourhood Warden Schemes: An overview**. Jessica Jacobson and Esther Saville. 2000.

3. **Alcohol and Crime: Taking stock.** Ann Deehan. 1999.

4. (Awaiting publication) However, 12 briefing notes under the general title **Reducing Domestic Violence ... What works?** have been published in advance of this publication. 2000.

5. **RV Snapshot: UK policing and repeat victimisation**. Graham Farrell, Alan Edmunds, Louise Hobbs and Gloria Laycock. 2000.